Pat Sloan's

Teach Me to Make
My First Quilt

A How-To Book for
All You Need to Know

Martingale
Create with Confidence

Pat Sloan's Teach Me to Make My First Quilt:
A How-To Book for All You Need to Know
© 2017 by Pat Sloan

Martingale®
19021 120th Ave. NE, Ste. 102
Bothell, WA 98011-9511 USA
ShopMartingale.com

Printed in Hong Kong
22 21 20   8 7 6 5 4 3

Library of Congress Cataloging-in-Publication Data is available upon request.

ISBN: 978-1-60468-827-6

MISSION STATEMENT

We empower makers who use fabric and yarn
to make life more enjoyable.

CREDITS

PUBLISHER AND
CHIEF VISIONARY OFFICER
Jennifer Erbe Keltner

CONTENT DIRECTOR
Karen Costello Soltys

DESIGN MANAGER
Adrienne Smitke

MANAGING EDITOR
Tina Cook

COVER AND
INTERIOR DESIGNER
Regina Girard

ACQUISITIONS EDITOR
Karen M. Burns

PHOTOGRAPHER
Brent Kane

TECHNICAL EDITOR
Nancy Mahoney

ILLUSTRATOR
Lisa Lauch

COPY EDITOR
Sheila Chapman Ryan

— CONTENTS —

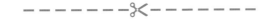

Let's Make the Blocks

Let's Make Our First Quilt

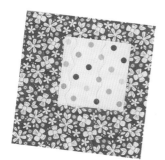

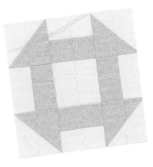

There's more online!

Find instructions to make a sampler quilt based on the blocks in this book at ShopMartingale.com/extras!

In the first quilting class I ever took, we were taught to make quilts all by hand, no sewing machines. So we cut shapes with scissors using cardboard templates and hand pieced the blocks. Then, we hand quilted the entire quilt. Learning to make quilts this way taught me a lot of basic skills. I learned how a block goes together, why points get chopped off, why blocks sometimes finish at the wrong size, and how to fix simple stitching errors.

Let's fast-forward to you. You picked up this book because you want to learn to make a quilt. I've fine-tuned what you need to know so you'll be successful—and also so you'll have fun making a quilt.

Over the years I've taught many beginners, as well as quilters of all levels, different techniques. These techniques are the groundwork that will let you create amazing projects. This knowledge will also give you the confidence to tackle more difficult quilting projects with an understanding of how things work. Knowing the whys and hows of basic quiltmaking will give you the groundwork to make quilting enjoyable for a lifetime.

I want you to use this book so often that it becomes a good friend. Take notes in it; refer back to its pages; make it your handbook on a new and exciting quiltmaking adventure.

Now let's go sew!
~ Pat

To make your first quilt, you'll need a few basic tools. And of course fabric! For more on choosing and preparing fabric, go to page 12.

- - - - - - - ✀ - - - - - - -

Your Sewing Machine

You'll be learning to make quilt blocks and projects using a sewing machine. There are a few machine features that make it much easier to create a quilt. Let's get familiar with them.

♦ ¼" presser foot. All of your patchwork will be sewn using a ¼" seam allowance, and accuracy is important. To make this easier, a ¼" presser foot is available for most machines. Later we'll test to be sure you have an accurate ¼" seam allowance (see page 18). Even if you're using a special foot, make sure it's accurate.

♦ Lines on throat plate. The throat plate on many sewing machines has guidelines for sewing different seam-allowance widths. Many machines have a ¼" guideline. If your machine doesn't

have one, you can mark your throat plate with painter's tape.

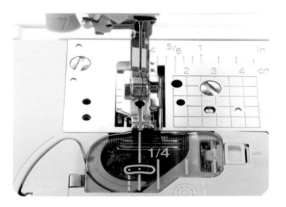

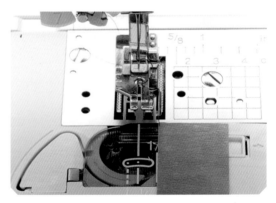

♦ Speed control. Your machine may have a sliding knob or dial that lets you adjust the sewing speed. Try sewing at full speed. Then set your machine to sew at half speed. Lastly, sew at the slowest speed. Determine which speed gives you the most control. You may feel you have more control with a lower speed. Setting the speed control allows you to press down fully on the foot pedal without losing control of your sewing.

- **Needle-down position.** There are many times when being able to stop with the needle in the down position helps you control your sewing. Use the needle-down position when machine appliquéing and quilting so you can pivot as needed without having the fabric move out of place. When piecing long seams, use the needle down position to maintain an accurate seam allowance.

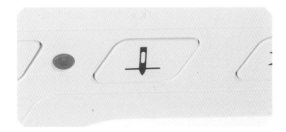

- **Walking foot or dual-feed foot.** A walking foot or dual-feed foot is a valuable tool when machine quilting the three layers of a quilt together (quilt top, batting, and backing) and when attaching binding. The layers in a quilt sandwich are thick, and a walking foot will evenly feed the quilt layers under the needle.

What Are Feed Dogs?

The feed dogs on your machine are the parallel set of jagged teeth that move back and forth as you sew.

Clean Your Machine

It's important to regularly clean your sewing machine. Lint from the fabric, thread, and batting builds up in the feed dogs and bobbin area. Balls of lint and lint pads can prevent the machine from making beautiful stitches. At the end of each project, clean the machine following the manufacturer's directions.

Tools for Quilters

Quilters need some basic tools to create a quilt. Some you may already have, but there are a few specific tools for creating accurate patchwork that you'll want to purchase. Starting off with the right tools for the job makes any task easier.

- **Pins.** I like 2" flat-head flower pins. They're easy to hold, the pin shaft is smooth and slender, and they're cute! Test new pins to make sure they're free of burrs and to be certain they'll slide into fabric smoothly. If they catch, throw them away.

- **Pincushions.** When sewing at my machine, I like a magnetic bowl or tray to catch pins. When I'm sewing in the family room, car, or with my friends, I use a pincushion I can push a pin into for safekeeping.

- **Rotary cutter.** I highly recommend purchasing a quality rotary cutter. This is one tool you'll use over and over again. If you're unsure about the style, try out a few of your friends' cutters to see which you like best. My favorite is an Olfa rotary cutter because it's easy to expose the blade.

  Because a rotary cutter gets a lot of use, change the blade as soon as it feels dull or if it has a nick or burr that makes it skip threads. Don't wait to change the blade until you have to use extra pressure to cut through the fabric layers. A nice sharp blade makes cutting easy, rather than a chore. See "How to Change a Rotary-Cutter Blade" on page 9.

- **Rulers.** As with many other tools, you have a lot of options when it comes to rulers. You'll need a long ruler for cutting strips of fabric, and square rulers are very helpful for squaring up blocks. I recommend you purchase at least three ruler sizes to start:
  - 6½" × 24½" or 6½" × 18½"
  - 12½" × 12½"
  - 6½" × 6½"

  Choose your rulers by ease of use. Can you easily see the lines when the ruler is on top of fabric? Can you easily read the numbers? Does the ruler confuse you? If so, then look at another brand. If you can, borrow a few different brands from friends to try. Or, ask for a demonstration at your local quilt shop. That way you can see what works best for you before you buy.

- **Cutting mat.** Quilters cut fabric with a rotary cutter and ruler on a self-healing mat. Choose the largest mat you can afford and have space to use. If possible, choose a mat that measures at least 24" along one edge so you can easily cut across the width of folded fabric.

- **Scissors and snips.** You'll be using a rotary cutter for cutting patchwork shapes, but you'll need scissors and snips for trimming threads and cutting appliqués.
  - Snips or a small pair of scissor are handy for trimming threads
  - Lightweight, sharp, smooth-opening scissors are a good choice for cutting appliqué shapes and trimming extra batting and backing from a layered quilt.

- **Seam ripper.** Another tool you'll become familiar with is your seam ripper. One quick way to "unsew" a seam is to cut every third or fourth thread along the stitched line. Gently remove the first two stitches in the seamline and you can easily pop open the seam by separating the two fabrics. Brush off all the loose threads before resewing the seam.

- **Thread.** Always use a quality 100% cotton thread. Use the same thread on the top and in the bobbin of the machine.

- **Fabric marking pens.** You'll need to mark on the wrong side of the fabric for a few techniques. Test different pens or pencils to make sure you can easily draw on the fabric and that the line is visible.

- **Iron.** An iron is another important tool, but it doesn't have to be fancy. You want a dependable iron that stays hot and doesn't leak.

- **Safety pins.** When you layer your quilt top, batting, and backing for quilting, you'll use 1" safety pins, called basting pins, to pin the three layers together.

- **Painter's tape.** Painter's tape can be used for several things, such as a guide on your ruler, taping the quilt backing to a table, and making a seam guide on your machine if you need one. This type of tape won't leave any residue, so add a roll to your sewing kit.

- **Sewing-machine needles.** Use a Universal size 70/10 or 80/12 for piecing, machine appliqué, and machine quilting.

Needle Sizes

There are two needle sizing systems: American and European. American needle sizes range from 8 to 19 and European sizes range from 60 to 120. The larger the number, the larger the shaft of the needle. Often you'll see both sizing numbers on the needle package, such as 60/8 and 70/10. Packages labeled 130/705 H are for use in home sewing machines rather than industrial machines.

- **Hand-sewing needles.** Sharps or milliner's needles (also called straw needles) are great for hand sewing binding in place. Get a variety package of needles that range in size from 9 to 12 to try out to see which works best for you.

When to Change the Needle

Listen to the sound the needle makes as you sew. When the needle is dull, you'll hear the needle thumping or punching through the fabric, which means it's time to change the needle. I recommend buying large packages of needles. Not only will you save money, but you can freely change the needle whenever you need to.

◆ Batting. Batting can be purchased in several sizes, from crib to king size. You'll also find it on bolts at your favorite quilt shop. If you want your washed quilt to have a more crinkled, aged look, use a 100% cotton batting. If you prefer a smoother looking quilt after it's washed, use a blended batting that's 80% cotton and 20% polyester.

How to Change a Rotary-Cutter Blade

It's not hard to change the blade, but do it carefully so you don't cut yourself. Assembly may vary from brand to brand, so pay attention to the order in which you remove the parts so you can reassemble them in the correct order.

1. Remove the back screw and lay the pieces out as shown, keeping them in order and placing them in the direction they will go back onto the cutter. Note the curved washer is curved *up* toward you.

2. Carefully lift off the blade and put it into a used blade case before discarding.

3. Place a new blade on your cutter handle and reassemble the components. You'll notice that replacement blades for rotary cutters come packaged slightly oily. This excess oil is part of the manufacturing process and should be wiped off, but don't wipe the blade clean. A little oil will help keep your blade rolling smoothly in your cutter.

4. Test the cutter on a scrap piece of fabric to be sure it's assembled correctly and the blade rolls smoothly. If you screw the mechanism too tightly, the blade won't roll smoothly, but if it's too loose, the blade could wobble.

Common Quilting Terms

Like any hobby or craft, making a quilt comes with its own set of terminology. Some of it can be a little confusing, especially since the word *quilt* can be a noun (the finished item) or a verb (the act of sewing the layers together to make a quilt). So don't be confused if you hear someone say that they want to *quilt their own quilt*. Once you understand the basic terms and some commonly used acronyms, you'll be up to speed on quilt lingo!

Appliqué. Fabric shapes stitched to the right side of a block or quilt.

Basting. The process of holding the top, batting, and backing together. Basting can be done with pins, thread, or temporary adhesive sprays.

Bias. Fabric cut at 45° angle from the straight of grain. True bias has the most stretch.

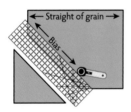

Chain piecing. Machine sewing units one right after the other without cutting the thread between the units saves time and thread.

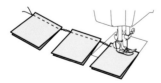

Crosscut. The process of sub-cutting strips into squares and rectangles.

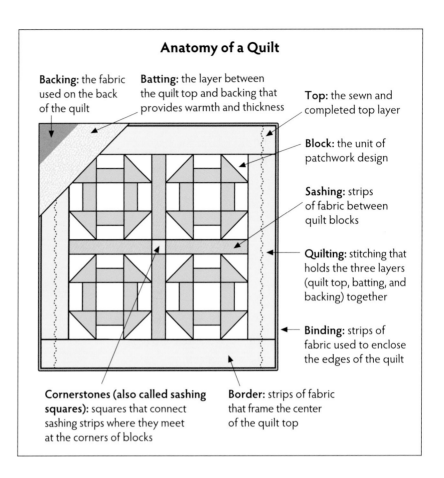

Anatomy of a Quilt

Backing: the fabric used on the back of the quilt

Batting: the layer between the quilt top and backing that provides warmth and thickness

Top: the sewn and completed top layer

Block: the unit of patchwork design

Sashing: strips of fabric between quilt blocks

Quilting: stitching that holds the three layers (quilt top, batting, and backing) together

Binding: strips of fabric used to enclose the edges of the quilt

Cornerstones (also called sashing squares): squares that connect sashing strips where they meet at the corners of blocks

Border: strips of fabric that frame the center of the quilt top

Fat eighth. A piece of fabric that measures 9" × 21". Fat eighths are often more useful than a normal eighth yard of fabric, which measures 4½" × 42", because of the extra width.

Fat quarter. A piece of fabric that measures 18" × 21". Fat quarters are handy for many types of quilts because they're wider than a normal quarter yard of fabric, which measures 9" × 42".

Finished size. The size of a block, not including the outer seam allowances. A block not yet stitched to any others will have a ¼" seam allowance all the way around it. For example, a 12" block will actually measure 12½" (12" + ¼" + ¼" = 12½") before it's joined to other blocks. The same block will measure 12" × 12" (the finished size) when sewn into a quilt.

Fussy cutting. Cutting patchwork to take advantage of an image printed on the fabric, such as centering a flower in the middle of a square.

Grain line. The direction of the straight lines of threads in the fabric, also called straight of grain. *Crosswise* grain runs across the width of the fabric, from selvage to selvage. This grain has a little bit of stretch. *Lengthwise* grain runs parallel to the selvage and has the least amount of stretch or give.

Half-square triangles. Cutting a square in half diagonally creates two half-square triangles. Also used to refer to a stitched unit made of two different half-square triangles.

Half-square triangles   Half-square triangle unit

Piecing. Sewing together pieces, units, or blocks using a ¼" seam allowance.

Quarter-square triangles. Cutting a square into quarters diagonally creates four quarter-square triangles. Also used to refer to a stitched unit made of four different quarter-square triangles.

Quarter-square triangles   Quarter-square triangle unit

Quilt block. A quilt block is one unit of a quilt. It's composed of smaller pieces (such as squares, rectangles, and triangles).

Quilt guild. A group of like-minded quilters that meets on a regular basis, similar to a club.

Quilt sandwich. Three layers (quilt top, batting, and backing) basted together.

Quilt shop. A retail store that carries fabric and tools used to make quilts.

Quilt top. The top layer of a quilt.

Quilting. The process of making a quilt, and also the stitching that holds the three layers together.

Selvage. The tightly woven edges of a fabric. One side usually has the fabric manufacturer's name, designer name, and color dots. These edges are created as the fabric is woven.

Squaring up. Making sure that a quilt block or quilt top is the correct size and has straight edges as well as right angles at every corner.

Stiletto. A tool that helps you grab and adjust fabric as you stitch. Use it to prevent the fabric from shifting, while keeping your fingers away from harm.

Strip piecing. Sewing strips of fabric together side by side. The resulting strip set can then be cut apart and the pieces sewn together or to other fabric units.

Unit. Individual pieces (such as squares, rectangles, and triangles) that are sewn together to make a block or quilt top.

Reading a Pattern

Quilt patterns are much like a recipe: there are ingredients (the materials list) followed by directions for making the dish (the quilt instructions), often given in steps. As you work through the projects, you'll build your skills for reading directions as you become familiar with how a quilt is made. Below are a few basics about reading patterns.

♦ **Project size.** The finished size of the project is listed on the first page of the instructions. When listing dimensions, the *x* is used to mean *by*, so 24½" × 24½" means 24½" square.

♦ **Block size.** The finished size of the block will also be listed on the first page of the instructions. (See "Block Size" on page 19.)

♦ **Materials.** A list of the fabrics you need to purchase to make the block or project. Each yardage amount is followed by the fabric color and a fabric letter (I've assigned each piece of fabric a letter for clarity as you're cutting and sewing).

♦ **Cutting.** Each fabric is listed by color and fabric letter, followed by what you need to cut from that particular fabric.

♦ **Assembly directions.** The first set of step-by-step instructions is for making the blocks. The next set of instructions is for sewing the blocks together and adding borders, if applicable.

♦ **Finishing directions.** Instructions for making the quilt sandwich, information about how I quilted my project, and binding instructions.

Let's face it: a quilt is all about sewing with fabric you love. Choosing fabric for your project is fun, but at first it might be a bit confusing. To give yourself a starting point, consider matching your quilt to your home decor or having the fabrics tell a story, such as using holiday colors for a Christmas quilt or wedding colors for an anniversary quilt.

Choosing Fabrics

For all of the projects for this book, I use a limited number of fabrics. This will help you see how different prints and colors look when cut up into small pieces and sewn back together. The more often you select and use fabric, the better you'll become at visualizing how the final quilt block and quilt will look.

"Let's Make the Blocks" (page 38) contains instructions for making nine different quilt blocks. The instructions for each block tell you the fabric pieces to cut to make the block. Then the project instructions in "Let's Make Our First Quilt" (page 65) tell you how much you'll need of each fabric to make the entire project. For example, in the Nine Patch project there are five fabrics: two for the blocks, one for the sashing, one for the sashing squares, and one for the border.

- On page 44, you'll find the block made in one color scheme, with the fabrics labeled A and B.

- The project instructions on page 74 list the fabric letters and how much of each fabric to purchase for the entire project. The project sample is made in different colors from the block.

Seeing the same block in different color combinations will help you visualize fabric placement.

Prewashing Fabric

I used 100% cotton quilting fabric for all the projects in this book. Before cutting, I recommend washing the fabric using cool water and a gentle soap. Tumble dry the fabric in your dryer on a normal setting. Remove the fabric from the dryer and press. Prewashing your fabrics will remove any excess dyes so that you won't have to worry about the dyes running or bleeding when you wash the finished quilt.

Cutting Fabric

For the projects in this book, you'll be cutting strips across the width of the fabric, and then crosscutting those strips into squares and rectangles. In following sections, you'll learn how to safely use a rotary cutter, how to hold the ruler correctly, and the best ways to cut particular shapes. Always cut on a rotary-cutting mat, not directly on the table. We used a gray mat for the photos in this book.

HOW TO USE A ROTARY CUTTER

- **Rotary cutters** have revolutionized quiltmaking, adding speed and accuracy to the cutting process. Always remember they are sharp and can be dangerous if not handled properly.

- **Keep the blade in the closed position** when not in use; this means *every time you put the cutter down*—even if it's just to reposition the fabric.

- **Hold the cutter correctly.** Let the cutter rest in the palm of your hand, slightly extend your index finger forward (it will help balance the cutter when you use it), and wrap your other three fingers and thumb around the handle.

- **Always cut *away* from your body.** Besides being safer, you have greater strength and accuracy when pushing the blade rather than pulling.

- **Keep all fingers of your noncutting hand firmly** on the ruler and well out of the way of the cutter.

- **When you start cutting,** hold the cutter in an upright position, not at an angle. Butt the cutter up next to the ruler and apply light pressure to cut against the ruler.

HOW TO HOLD A RULER

First, place your noncutting hand on the ruler, making sure all of your fingers are on the ruler, not over the edge. Separate your fingers a bit, sort of like a spider, so you have a better hold on the ruler.

To start, your noncutting hand should be just below the midpoint on your ruler. Keeping light pressure on the ruler, start cutting the fabric at the fold. As the rotary cutter reaches where your hand rests on the ruler, stop cutting. Without moving the rotary cutter, reposition your noncutting hand toward the top of the ruler. Then finish your cut.

To get used to the motion, cut practice fabric into strips so you get the feel for the ruler and

rotary cutter working together. Soon you won't even think about it!

PREPARING TO CUT

Before cutting a strip from a 42"-wide piece of fabric, it's important to make sure the fabric is folded properly so you don't end up with weird bends at the fold. Luckily this is super easy to do and only takes a minute.

Fabric in stores is folded lengthwise and 10 to 15 yard lengths are wound onto a piece of cardboard, called a *bolt* of fabric. The factory process of folding and winding the fabric can sometime cause the fabric to twist out of alignment. You need to make sure the grain is straight before cutting the fabric into pieces for your quilt.

1. **Press the fabric** so that it's smooth and wrinkle free.

2. **Fold the fabric,** wrong sides together, with the selvage edges aligned. If the fabric was cut off grain, wrinkles might appear. If they do, shift the selvage edges in opposite directions until the wrinkles disappear along the fold. Don't worry about lining up the raw edges of the fabric, but focus on lining up the selvage edges so the fabric is smooth.

Selvage edges

Raw edges

3. Lay the fabric on the cutting mat with the folded edge toward you. The raw edges may be uneven. That's OK—you'll trim off those edges before you cut the pieces for your project.

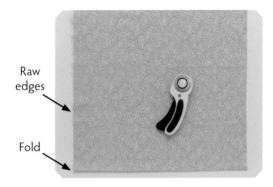

Raw edges

Fold

HOW TO MAKE A CLEANUP CUT

1. Align a horizontal line on a 6½" square ruler on the fold of the fabric with the ruler a bit inside the left edge.

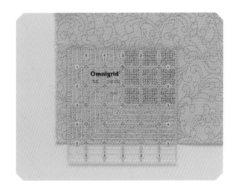

2. Place a 24½"-long ruler against the left side of the small ruler. The rulers should be only as far in from the raw edges as needed to cut through both layers of fabric. The top and bottom of the long ruler should extend beyond the fabric.

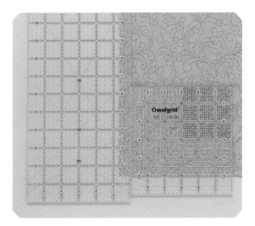

Left-Handed Quilters

The instructions and photos are for right-handed quilters. If you're left-handed, reverse the instructions.

3. Move the small ruler out of the way and hold the long ruler in place with your noncutting hand. Starting at the fold, make your cut by sliding the cutter away from you along the long edge of the ruler. Discard the fabric slivers. Now you're ready to cut strips for your project.

Using a Smaller Mat

If your cutting mat doesn't measure at least 24" along one edge, you can make a second fold in your fabric. Carefully fold the fabric in half lengthwise and align the first fold with the selvage edges. Place the folded fabric on the cutting mat with second fold at the bottom, closest to you. The first fold and selvages will be at the top. I recommend pressing firmly on the ruler and cutter as you cut through the four layers. Be sure your rotary-cutter blade is sharp.

HOW TO CUT LONG STRIPS

1. Place the long ruler on the fabric and measure in from the cut edge the width that you want your strip to be. If you want a 2½"-wide strip, align the 2½" line on the ruler with the cut edge of the fabric. One of the horizontal lines on the ruler should be perfectly aligned with the folded edge of the fabric. If it's not, your strip won't be totally straight.

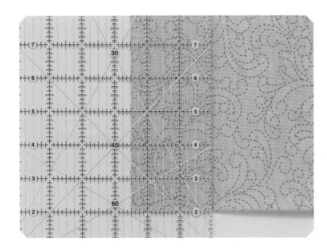

Keeping Track

If you're having trouble keeping track of the line on your ruler, use painter's tape to mark the entire length you're going to use.

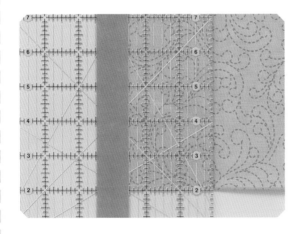

2. Cut along the edge of the ruler and open up the strip. Check to make sure that the strip is straight and not bent into a V shape at the fold. If the strip isn't straight, repeat steps 1–3 of "How to Make a Cleanup Cut" (page 14) to trim your fabric so that the fold is parallel to the selvage edge.

Use the Lines on the Ruler

I recommend using the lines on the ruler rather than the ones on the cutting mat. The lines on the ruler are more accurate than the lines on the mat. Besides that, if you follow the lines on the mat, you'll continually cut at the same spot all the time and that wears a groove into the mat. Grooves make the mats harder to use. Since you don't need the lines on the mat as a cutting guide, turn the mat to the plain side. You can easily cut on both sides of the mat and extend the life of your mat.

3. Continue cutting strips in the same manner, sliding your ruler the distance needed to cut the appropriate strip width. Check after every three or four strips to be certain you're still cutting perpendicular to the fold. After cutting a few strips you may need to make a cleanup cut to straighten the edge of the fabric again.

HOW TO CUT SQUARES AND RECTANGLES

If you're planning to cut shapes from strips, leave the strips folded. When cutting the shapes from a folded strip, you'll get two from each cut you make. In this book, all cutting instructions include a ¼" seam allowance.

1. **To cut a square or rectangle,** begin by cutting strips of the appropriate width.

2. **Place the strip of fabric horizontally** on the cutting mat. Place a line on the ruler on the edge of the strip. Trim off the end of the strip to remove the selvages and to square up the ends of the strip.

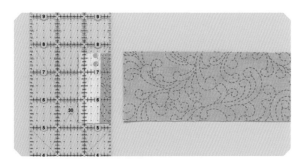

3. **To cut squares,** find the measurement on the ruler that corresponds with the width of the strip. Below, we're cutting 2½" squares. Align the vertical line with the clean-cut edge of the strip. Cut through both layers of fabric. Cut as many squares as the length allows, or as many as you need for the project you're making.

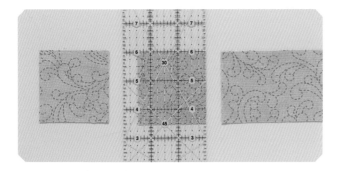

4. **To cut rectangles,** cut the desired length, making sure the horizontal and vertical lines are aligned with the cut edges of the strip. Cut through both layers of fabric. Cut as many rectangles as the length allows, or as many as you need for the project you're making.

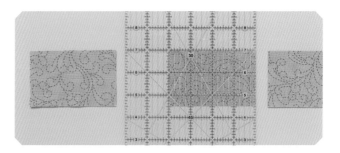

Slice Off the Selvages

It's best to not include selvage in your patchwork. Because the selvages are attached to the machinery, they are more tightly woven than the rest of the fabric and they may or may not be printed with the fabric's design. If you use pieces that contain the selvage, the tight weave can cause the patchwork unit to be the wrong size if the selvage is fairly thick.

When you're first learning a new task, it feels like everything is happening at once. Much like driving a car, when sewing you have to think about several things at the same time. So let's take it slow, one thing at a time. We'll start with sewing a straight line.

– – – – – – – ✂ – – – – – – –

Sewing a Straight Line

Here are five tips for sewing straight lines.

♦ **Get the right position.** Your arms should be at a 90° or right angle to the bed of the machine. Ergonomically, this is the most comfortable position so your shoulders don't ache and your neck won't hurt. Don't sit too close to your machine; you should be able to look down and see the needle.

♦ **A seam guideline is the key** to success. A straight line really means a consistent seam allowance. When sewing two pieces of fabric together, the area to the right of the stitched line is the seam allowance. Whether you're sewing squares or 2½" × 42" strips together, you want the seam allowance to be the same from start to finish. Your machine has a seam-allowance guideline. If you feel it's too short and not helpful, then extend the guideline with painter's tape so you can see it along the entire bed of your sewing machine.

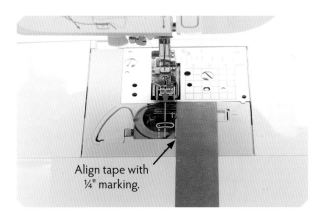

Align tape with ¼" marking.

♦ **Watch your pace.** Just like driving, learn to finesse the foot pedal so you have a constant speed. If you're struggling with maintaining a constant pace, then turn down the speed control so you can't go too fast.

♦ **Don't watch the needle.** Always look in front of the needle so you can see where you're going. Keep an eye on the edge of the fabric, making sure it stays lined up on your seam guideline.

♦ **The *P* word: Practice!** The more you sew, the easier it becomes. And many things will become second nature so you won't even think about them, just like when you're driving.

Sewing a ¼" Seam Allowance

Sewing a consistent ¼"-wide seam allowance is very important in quiltmaking. Quilt blocks are generally building blocks of specific-sized squares, rectangles, and sometimes other shapes that fit together like a puzzle to create the final block in a specific size. And like a puzzle, if a piece is the wrong size, it won't fit in its spot.

If your seam allowance is *less* than ¼", your units (or blocks) will be too big and your seam intersections won't match. If your seam allowance is *greater* than ¼", your units (or blocks) will be too small, and once again, your seam intersections won't match up and the final block will be the wrong size.

Even if you use a ¼" foot on your machine, you need to be sure you're sewing an accurate ¼" seam allowance. Here's an easy test to see if your seam allowance is accurate.

1. Cut two matching light 2½" squares and one dark 2½" square.

2. Sew the light squares to opposite sides of the dark square. Press the seam allowances toward the dark square.

3. Measure the dark square *from seam to seam*. It should be 2" wide. If the measurement is less than 2", then your seam allowance is too wide and you need to make a narrower seam allowance. If the measurement is wider than 2", your seam allowance is too narrow and you need to make it wider.

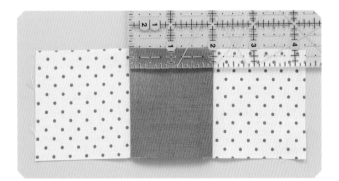

Fixing an Inaccurate Seam Allowance

Place a small ruler (one with markings in ¼" increments) under the needle on your sewing machine. *Slowly* lower the needle by turning the flywheel by hand, until it barely touches the ruler. Adjust the ruler until the needle is on the ¼" line on the ruler and the edge of the ruler is ¼" to the right of the needle. Where is the ruler in relation to the seam guideline on your machine? Is it spot on? If not, you need to make some adjustments.

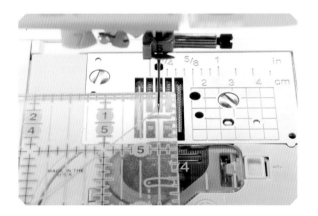

If your seam allowance is too wide, raise the needle slightly. Using the needle-position button on your machine, move the needle one position to the *right*. Carefully lower the needle and align it with the ¼" line on the ruler. If needed, repeat to move the needle one more position to the right.

If your seam allowance is too narrow, raise the needle slightly. Using the needle-position button on your machine, move the needle one position to the *left*. Carefully lower the needle and align it with the ¼" line on the ruler. If needed, repeat to move the needle one more position to the left.

Sometimes you simply can't adjust the needle to match the seam guideline on the machine, because either you're unable to move the needle to the correct position or your machine doesn't have a needle-position button. In that case, place a piece of painter's tape on the machine along the right side of the ruler to make your own seam guideline that you can follow.

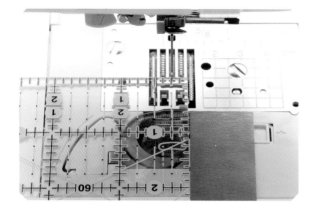

Recheck your seam allowance whenever you sew on a new machine, or if your blocks are not coming out the right size. Sometimes our minds wander and we're no longer following the seam guideline.

Block Size

You'll often see blocks described as a 12" block or a 9" block. The standard way to refer to a block is to give the *finished* size, which doesn't include the outer seam allowances. That's the size the block will be after it's sewn together with other blocks, sashing, or a border.

So what size is the block after it's made but before it's sewn next to something? Let's use a 12" square finished block as an example. Before a block is sewn into a quilt, it has a ¼" seam allowance all the way around the outer edges. That means your block is 12½" square, including the seam allowances. Here is the math: 12" + ¼" + ¼" = 12½".

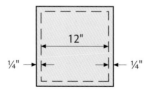

This formula works anytime you want to determine the size of a unit or block. Let's say

you've sewn a 2½" square to another 2½" square. Following is the simple formula.

♦ The *finished* size of both squares is 2". After sewing the squares together, the finished width of the unit is 4" (2" + 2" = 4"). The finished unit is 2" tall.

♦ To determine the size of the sewn unit, *including* the seam allowances, add ½" to the width and height of the unit. The formula would be 4" + ¼" + ¼" = 4½" and 2" + ¼" + ¼" = 2½". Therefore, the size of the unit (including the seam allowances) would be 4½" wide × 2½" tall.

Being able to do this simple formula lets you quickly check that your seam allowance is accurate and that the size of the unit you're sewing is correct.

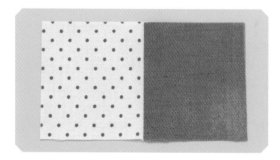

Grid-Based Blocks

Most patchwork quilt blocks (as opposed to appliquéd shapes) are based on a grid system. Think of the grid as a piece of graph paper. If the squares on the graph paper are equivalent to 1" × 1", then a 2" square covers two across and two down. The grid system allows us to easily see how to sew pieces into units and then sew the units together to make a block.

Basic Sewing Order

For each block in this book, I'll show you the sewing order to make the block. Here's the basic sewing order you'll follow.

Make units. You'll start by sewing squares or rectangles together to make a unit. You'll either add another fabric piece to the unit, or you'll sew the unit to another unit of the same size.

Check the unit size. After making a unit, be sure to check the size. The correct size of the unit, including seam allowances, will be listed in each step.

Sew the completed units together. Line up the units (or fabric pieces) so the ends and seam intersections match. You'll immediately notice if your units are not the correct size. If the units are too big or too small, they won't line up correctly.

It's important to press the seam allowances so they meet or nestle against each other at the seam intersections. That way you'll reduce the fabric bulk you're sewing over where the seams meet, and it will be easier for the pieces to match up.

Using a Four Patch as an example, the sewing order would be as follows.

1. Lay out two light and two dark same-sized squares. Join the squares into two rows of two squares each as shown. Press the seam allowances toward the dark square in each row (see "Pressing" on page 22).

2. Lay one row on top of the other, right sides together. Since the seam allowances are pressed in opposite directions, the ends of the rows should be even on both sides when the seam allowances are matched up. Pin the seam intersection and the ends of the row in place.

3. Whenever possible, position the unit with the top seam allowance pointing toward the needle. That way, the presser foot will push the top fabric a bit and it will nestle into the fabric on the bottom. Join the pieces with a straight seam using a ¼" seam allowance.

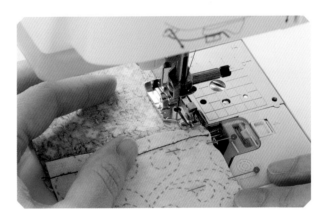

4. Press the seam allowances of the completed unit in one direction as described in "Pressing."

Using a Starter Square

Whenever you're sewing small squares or narrow rectangles, it helps to begin (and end) all of your seams on a scrap piece of fabric that I call a starter square. Beginning with a starter square keeps the feed dogs from "eating" the top edges of the fabric when you start stitching. (The feed dogs on your machine are the parallel set of jagged teeth that move back and forth to move the fabric as you sew.)

Here's how to use a starter square.

1. **Fold a 2" square in half,** either right sides together or wrong sides together. Place the folded square under the presser foot and sew to the edge of the starter square.

2. **Layer the two pieces** you're sewing right sides together and place them at the front of the presser foot. The right edges of the pieces should be aligned with the seam guideline.

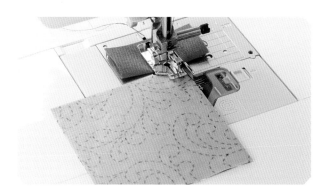

3. **Sew the seam.** As you get toward the end, be sure you don't shift away from the seam guideline. (I find many people don't keep the patches on the guideline all the way to the end.) If you shift off the seam guideline, your seam allowance won't be accurate the whole length of the seam.

4. **Sew off of the patches** onto your starter square. If you're chain piecing (below), sew onto the starter square after joining the last pieces.

Chain Piecing

One of the quilting terms you'll start hearing almost right away is *chain piecing.* Chain piecing is an assembly-line method that lets you sew pieces together quickly. Often you'll need to sew many of the same pieces together to make a quilt. If you cut pieces and stack them into groups, then you can sit and sew the pieces together one right after the other, creating a chain of sewn units that aren't clipped apart until after they're all sewn.

To chain piece, feed the first pair of patches under the presser foot.

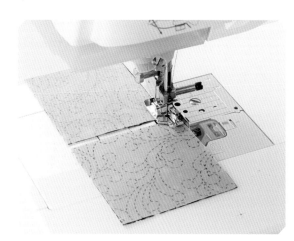

Continue feeding patches through the machine without cutting the thread. After you finish sewing the last one, cut the chain to remove the pieces from the machine, leaving the starter square under the machine needle.

I recommend chain piecing because it will save time. You don't have to stop, pull the patchwork out, and trim the thread after every pair is sewn. Chain piecing will also save thread. You use less thread between chain-pieced patches than you do if you pull the patchwork out of the machine and trim the long tails every time.

Pressing

Pressing as you stitch is just as important as checking the block size after sewing each seam. Pressing allows you to be sure that when you sew one unit to another, all the pieces are flat. You've basically made a new piece of fabric and you don't want it to be wrinkled. You also don't want to have folds, pleats, or tucks along the seamline. If the seam is not fully pressed, the fold or tuck will make the block smaller. It may seem time-consuming to press so often, but in the beginning I recommend you press after sewing every seam. It will let you see the block as it develops, and will also give you the most accurate results.

To steam or not to steam, that is the question! All quilters must decide what works best for them. If you don't use steam, you may find that a fabric doesn't have a crisp crease. I recommend trying both steam and no steam to see how it works for you. I personally use steam.

Pressing is an up and down motion. Don't push the iron back and forth over the patchwork; you might stretch the units out of shape. I recommend pressing like this.

1. **While the unit is closed,** press the seam allowances to warm up the fibers.

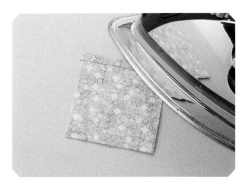

2. **Flip one piece over** so you see the right side of the patchwork. When possible, flip open the darker fabric. If you can't press toward the darker fabric, then press in a direction that allows you to butt up the seam allowances when sewing one unit to another.

3. **Press the seam from the right side,** making sure the piece is totally folded over and there's no crease along the seamline.

Whenever you need to press the seam allowances toward the lighter fabric, check that you can't see the seam allowance of the darker fabric peeking out from behind the lighter seam allowance. That is called shadowing. To fix any shadowing, carefully trim the darker seam allowance just a little bit so it's not showing.

Squaring Up Blocks

Once the block is completed, it's time for a last check of the block's size. All the blocks in this book are 12" square finished, which means they should measure 12½" square with the outer seam allowances included. Use the following method to make sure the block measures 12½" square.

USING A SQUARE RULER

A 12½" square ruler is a great investment. It can be used for squaring up blocks, squaring up a quilt top, and cutting strips, rectangles, and squares.

1. To find the center of a 12½" square ruler, divide 12½" by 2, which equals 6¼" (12½ ÷ 2 = 6¼). Therefore, the center of the ruler is the intersection of the horizontal and vertical 6¼" lines.

Mark the Center

Draw an arrow on a small sticky note. Place the sticky note on the ruler, with the arrow pointing to the center spot.

2. Find the center of your quilt block. On a 12½" block, the center point would be 6¼". The center of a Four Patch block is where the four squares meet. The center of a Nine Patch block is the middle of the center square.

3. Fold the block in half in both directions and finger press.

4. Place the square ruler on top of the block, with the center of the ruler aligned with the center of the block. Make sure the ruler is straight and covers the block. The edges of the 12½" square ruler should be even with the edges of the 12½" block, and none of the block should be showing beyond the ruler. If the edges of your block aren't aligned with the ruler, don't worry. Turn to "Fixing Block-Size Errors" on page 24 for solutions.

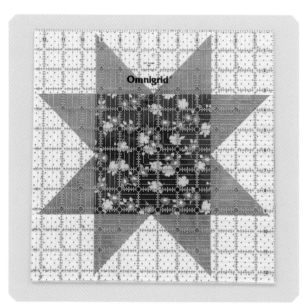

Trim the Dog-Ears

When trimming blocks and units, you'll also trim off the *dog-ear* triangles. Removing the dog-ears makes sewing blocks and units together so much easier!

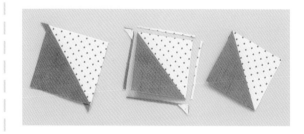

FIXING BLOCK-SIZE ERRORS

Sometimes the block is not the right size. The block might be too small, or too big, all the way around. Or, it might be short or long on just one side, so if you shifted the ruler off of center, the block is the right size, but it's not centered with the ruler.

While you're learning to make blocks, I recommend you take the time to figure out what went wrong. You can work with a block that's a fraction off, but if your block is ¼" or more off, or way off center, now is the time to fix it. It won't improve as you go along; the error will only increase as you keep adding blocks to your quilt. The blocks won't fit and it will be frustrating.

Using a Nine Patch block (like the one on page 44) that measures 12½" square including seam allowances as an example, here's how to figure out why your block is not the correct size.

- Flip the block over and look at the seams. Can you quickly spot where some seam allowances might be too small, too large, or inconsistent? Seam-allowance errors result in a patchwork unit that's the incorrect size, which is why the block is not the correct size.

- To the right of the center mark, does your block measure 6¼"? If not, a patchwork seam or cut square was incorrect on that side of the block. Check from the center in all directions so you know which side is the problem.

- Measure the center square. Since it's joined to other squares on all four sides, it should be 4" × 4". If it's not the correct size, then a seam needs to be corrected or the square wasn't cut correctly.

- Measure the four corner squares. Since they're sewn to other squares on *two* sides, they should be 4¼" × 4¼". If they aren't the correct size, then a seam needs to be corrected or a square wasn't cut correctly.

- Measure the four side squares; they should be 4" × 4¼". Why are they different? Because three of the sides are sewn to other squares, with a seam allowance on one side only. Again, if a square is not the correct size, a seam needs to be corrected or the square wasn't cut correctly.

- Once you've determined what needs to be corrected, it's time to get out your seam ripper and unsew.

Unsewing

Unsewing is the process of removing stitches and taking apart pieces that you've already sewn together. There will be times when you need to make a correction, and having a great seam ripper makes the process easier. Ripping out stitches shouldn't be hard or frustrating; it's just part of quiltmaking.

- Remove the stitches holding the patchwork in place.
- Take off all the loose threads.
- Press each piece flat again.
- Pin the pieces together.
- Sew the seam again.

Appliqué is simply the process of adding a fabric shape on top of another fabric. In this book, I'm going to show you one method of appliqué—fusible machine appliqué. There are many other appliqué methods you can explore later. This method will teach you how easy it is to add shapes to any project, and it's one of my very favorite things to do. Fusible web is a product that adheres two pieces of fabric together. Use your iron to melt the adhesive and fuse the pieces together; then stitch by machine around each fabric shape.

- - - - - - - ✂ - - - - - - -

Tools

- **Paper-backed fusible web.** A variety of fusible products are available, but my favorite is HeatnBond Lite because it's easy to use and very dependable.

- **Tracing Tool.** Either a pen or pencil works for tracing the shapes onto the paper side of the fusible web.

- **Scissors.** Pick a pair that's sharp and lightweight, with long blades. (You can use a rotary cutter when cutting straight lines.)

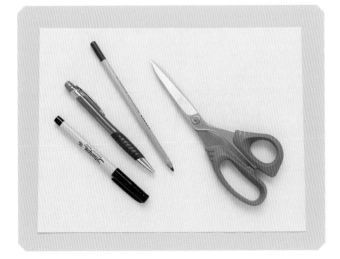

Preparing the Appliqué

1. **Place the fusible web** over the pattern, paper side up, and trace the shape onto the paper.

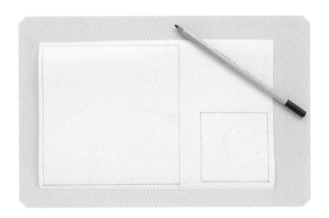

2. **Roughly cut out the shape,** leaving about ½" around the outside edges of the drawn line.

3. To avoid having too much fusible web in your appliqué shapes, which can make your quilt stiff, cut through the excess web around the shape, through the marked line, and into the interior of the shape. Then cut away the excess fusible web on the inside of the shape, leaving about ¼" of fusible web inside the drawn line.

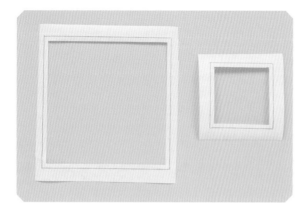

4. Lay the appropriate fabric on your ironing board, wrong side up. Position the fusible-web shape on the fabric, paper side facing up. Heat by pressing with your iron as instructed by the manufacturer. When you apply heat, the adhesive melts so it sticks to the fabric.

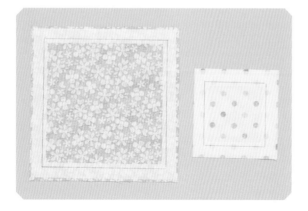

5. Cut on the marked line to create your final appliqué shape.

6. Remove the paper backing from each shape. If needed, fold the paper to make a crease and it will lift right off.

Fusing the Appliqué to the Background

1. Place the background fabric on your ironing board, right side up.

2. Place the appliqué shape on the background fabric with the adhesive side facing down.

3. Following the manufacturer's instructions, press with a hot iron to fuse the appliqué shape to the background. Do not press for longer than recommended or the adhesive may not hold.

Stitching the Appliqué

After fusing, you need to stitch around the appliqué shapes to secure them to the background fabric. Many quiltmakers use a blanket stitch to secure their fusible appliqués. If your machine doesn't have a blanket stitch, here are a couple other stitch options you can use. I used a straight stitch for all the appliqué shapes in this book.

Blanket stitch. Depending on your machine, you may have several different blanket-stitch options available. Any blanket-stitch option will work fine for my appliqué method.

Straight stitch. Sew a straight line, ⅛" inside the shape, to secure the shape to the background.

Zigzag stitch. Set your machine to make a narrow zigzag stitch. Zigzag around the edge of the shape to sew it to the background.

Blanket stitch   *Straight stitch*   *Zigzag stitch*

Find Out More

You can learn more about my fusible-appliqué techniques in my book *Pat Sloan's Teach Me to Appliqué* (Martingale, 2015).

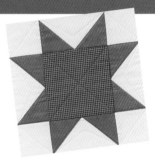

Once you've made all the blocks needed for your quilt top, then it's time to sew them together. In some quilts, the patchwork (or appliqué) blocks are sewn together side by side. In other designs, the instructions may call for sashing or use plain alternate blocks between the pieced blocks.

Simple Straight Set

In this traditional setting, blocks are set side by side. This is the type of setting I used in the Rail Fence Quilt (page 68).

1. **Arrange the blocks in rows** as shown in the quilt assembly diagram for your project.

2. **Sew the blocks together** in horizontal (or vertical) rows. Press the seam allowances in opposite directions from row to row.

3. **Pin the rows together,** being careful to match the seam intersections from row to row. Sew the rows together and press the seam allowances in one direction.

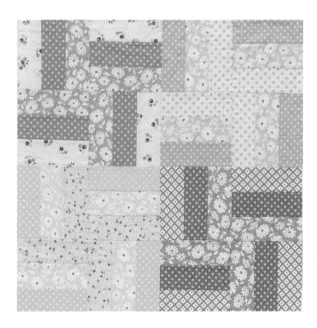

Rail Fence blocks, set side by side

Keeping Track

Once you've made all your blocks and arranged them into rows on a design wall, floor, or your bed, it's helpful to have a method for keeping track of the placement. That way you can sew the blocks together in the correct order.

Below are a couple methods for keeping track of the blocks.

- Take a photo with a digital camera. You can refer back to the photo as needed when joining the blocks.

- Label the rows and blocks with a note. For example, for row 1, block 1, write R1-B1. For row 1, block 2, write R1-B2. Pin the note to the *top* of each appropriate block. Then you can stack the blocks. If a block is out of order or is turned the wrong way, it doesn't matter because you can locate where the block goes and know which side is the top of the block!

Sashing

Sashing separates the blocks, giving a visual break between them. Sashing is a good option when you don't want to match points from block to block, such as the points in Sawtooth Star blocks (page 86). Sashing can add another element or color to the quilt and will make a project larger.

Before arranging the blocks and sashing in rows as shown in the quilt assembly diagram for your project, make sure the blocks match the size given for the sashing. If your sashing is cut 2" × 12½", that means your block should be 12½" square for the sashing to fit perfectly. If your blocks are larger or smaller than the sashing size, you need to fix your blocks so they're the correct size.

A common mistake people make is to increase the size of the sashing to match too-large blocks. When you do that you introduce a large error in the project size. And, if there are many blocks, the increased size could mean your quilt will not be square or even worse, the blocks won't fit together as you go along. It's much better to fix the blocks so they're the right size. Then you can assemble the quilt as instructed for your project.

Adding Borders

You're ready to add the final touch to your quilt top—borders! The way to make sure the borders are the correct size is measure the quilt top before you cut the borders. If you don't measure, you run the risk of the borders being uneven and rippling along the quilt edge. Just like with every other step, checking to make sure the blocks are square and are the correct size before you add the borders will give you a beautiful finished project. You also need to make sure the quilt top is square.

♦ **Lay the quilt top on a flat surface.** Place a square ruler on one corner. Use a yardstick or another ruler to extend the length. Check that the corner is perfectly square and the side of your quilt is straight. Repeat to check each corner and side of the quilt top.

♦ **If the quilt top is not square,** it means a block is not the correct size, or maybe your seam allowance was off when you joined the blocks or added the sashing. Perhaps the seam allowances went from narrow to wide. Somewhere, something is off. Look the top over and fix the issue before adding borders.

♦ **To find the correct measurement** for the border strips, always measure through the *center* of the quilt, not at the outside edges. This ensures that the borders are of equal length on opposite sides of the quilt and brings the outer edges in line with the center dimension.

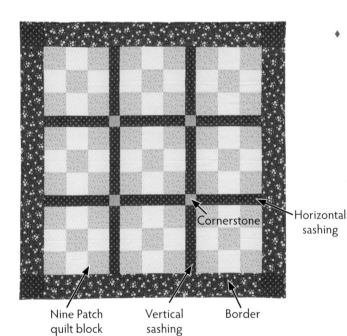

Nine Patch quilt block · Vertical sashing · Border · Cornerstone · Horizontal sashing

Nine Patch blocks set together with sashing and cornerstones

SIDE BORDERS

1. Measure the quilt top from top to bottom through the center. Cut two side border strips to this measurement.

2. Fold each border strip in half to find the center. Pin-mark the center of each strip.

3. Fold the quilt top in half to find the center along each side. Pin-mark the center.

4. With right sides together and aligning the raw edges, pin the borders to the sides of the quilt top, matching the centers and ends. Pin between the end and center with several pins, halving the distance each time. Repeat for the other half of the border. The edges of the quilt top and border should be flat, without any puckers.

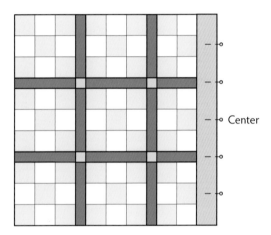

Center

5. Using a walking foot, sew the side borders in place. (The walking foot will help evenly feed the top and bottom fabrics as you sew.) Press the seam allowances toward the border strips.

TOP AND BOTTOM BORDERS

1. Measure the width of the quilt top from side to side through the center, including the side borders.

2. Repeat steps 2–5 of "Side Borders" to pin, sew, and press the top and bottom borders to the quilt.

Ruffly Borders

One problem you might encounter is that the quilt-top edges and the border are not the same size and are not lying flat. This can happen if your blocks are a little off or the border isn't cut correctly. Start by measuring the center of the quilt top and the length of the border strips again. If the border strips are not cut correctly, make the necessary adjustments.

If the border strips are the correct length, then the problem is the quilt top.

If the difference between the length of the quilt top and the border is greater than ½", you need to correct the issue. Look the quilt top over and fix the problem.

If the difference is ½" or less, generously pin to ease or slightly stretch the quilt top to fit the border. The border strips are the same length, so the edges will work out correctly.

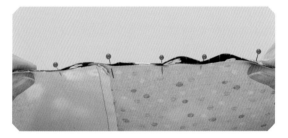

To ease a border to fit, match the midpoint of the border and quilt top and pin together. Also pin at each end. Then pin at the quarter points. Continue dividing the space evenly and pinning to distribute the difference in lengths. Sew with the longer piece on the bottom, where the feed dogs will work to your advantage!

It's time to turn your quilt top into a quilt. In this section you'll learn how to layer and baste the "quilt sandwich," and then quilt the layers together, add a label, and bind the quilt.

- - - - - - - ✂- - - - - - - -

Making the Quilt Backing

Starting with my first quilt, I made the backing using fabrics left over from the quilt top. If I didn't have leftover fabrics, I sometimes used fabrics that fell into the "I don't know why I bought them" category, so I could use them up! Now I prefer my backing to complement the front.

For smaller quilts, such as wall hangings and table runners, the backing should be 4" wider than the top, which allows at least 2" on all sides. Most fabric is about 40" wide, once you account for shrinkage and removing the selvages. Quilts less than 35" wide can use one length of fabric for the backing. For example, if a quilt top is 24½" × 24½", you would cut a piece of backing fabric that's 28½" × 28½" (24½" + 4" = 28½").

If the quilt is 35" or wider, you'll need to piece the backing. For large quilts, the backing should be 6" to 8" wider than the top, which allows 3" to 4" of backing on all sides for positioning the batting and top accurately.

Calculating Backing Fabric

Determining how much fabric you need for a backing sounds scary, but it's actually quite simple. Here's my formula.

- Add the extra inches needed for a quilting allowance (4" to 8") to both the width and length measurements of the quilt top. If both dimensions are less than 35", add 4" to both dimensions. If either dimension is 35" or larger (but less than 80"), add 6" to both dimensions. If either dimension is 80" or larger, add 8" to each dimension. For instance, if the quilt is 60" × 80", the backing fabric needs to be at least 68" × 88".

- Divide the width measurement of the quilt by the width of the backing fabric. Round up the result to the nearest whole number. In this instance, the equation would be as follows: 68" ÷ 40" = 1.7; round up to 2. The result is how many lengths of fabric you need.

- Multiply the length of the quilt by the number of fabric lengths you need. Divide the result by 36", and that equals the number of yards you need to buy. The calculation would be as follows: 88" × 2 lengths = 176". 176" ÷ 36" = 4.88 yards. So, you'll need 5 yards to back a 60" × 80" quilt. If you plan on prewashing the backing, add 10% for shrinkage (173 + 10% = 5.37 or 5⅜ yards).

If you're using just one fabric for the backing, you'll need to calculate how much backing fabric is required based on the width of the quilt top. For quilts that are 40" to 60" wide, use two lengths of fabric with one *horizontal* seam.

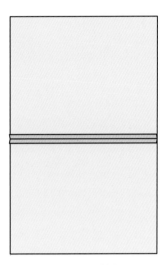

Two lengths of fabric
with a horizontal center seam

For quilts that are 60" to 72" wide, use two lengths of fabric with one *vertical* seam.

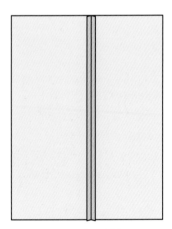

Two lengths of fabric
with a vertical center seam

For quilts wider than 72", use three lengths of fabric with two *horizontal* seams. If the quilt is square, the seam can be positioned horizontally or vertically.

BACKING YARDAGE			
Quilt Size	Dimensions	Backing	2¼" Binding
Twin	63" × 87"	5 yards	⅝ yard
Double	78" × 87"	7¼ yards	¾ yard
Queen	84" × 92"	7½ yards	¾ yard
King	100" × 92"	8¼ yards	⅞ yard

Layering and Basting

If you're going to use only one basting method, pin basting is the one to learn. I find pin basting is the easiest way to baste a quilt sandwich. You'll need the following:

♦ Lots of 1" safety pins

♦ Clamps (either quilters' clamps or office binder clamps)

1. **Lay the freshly pressed backing,** wrong side up, on a large, clean table. Smooth out all the wrinkles. Clamp the edges to the table about every 6" to 8", gently pulling the backing taut before clamping it in place. The object is to make sure the backing is smooth, flat, and wrinkle free, but to not stretch it out of shape.

2. **Center the batting** on top of the backing, patting it smooth and making sure the edges are parallel. Be careful not to tug and twist, just gently lift the batting up and down to place it straight on the back. If you're using a packaged batting that's been folded, take it out of the package the day before and lay it flat to let the creases relax before you start to baste. Or, place in the dryer and use the "air" setting to fluff out the creases.

3. **Center the pressed quilt top,** right side up, on the batting and backing. Check to be certain that both the backing and batting extend several inches past the quilt top on all sides. Smooth out any wrinkles, working from the center to the outer edges, again taking care not to stretch any part of the quilt out of shape.

4. **Starting in the center,** place pins every 4", or even closer. Place the pins in rows, working your way to the outer edges. Don't remove the clamps until the entire quilt is covered edge to edge with pins.

5. **Pin or machine baste** around the outer edges. Trim the batting, leaving 1" on all sides of the quilt top. When sewing, remove each pin before you come to it.

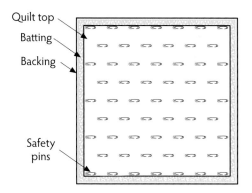

Quilt top
Batting
Backing
Safety pins

Walking-Foot Quilting

Most sewing machine come with a dual-feed presser foot called a walking foot. Some machines even have a built-in dual-feed system. A walking foot will evenly feed the thick quilt sandwich through your machine so you don't create puckers or pleats as you quilt the top, batting, and backing layers together. From quilting straight lines to decorative stitches, your walking foot offers lots of options.

Straight-line stitching. Quilting straight lines is a great way to start quilting your projects. This method can be simple, elegant, or even very detailed. Mainly, it gets the job done, which is to hold all the layers together so the quilt can be used.

Wavy lines and decorative stitching. Decorative stitches can add a fun look to your quilts. Look for decorative stitches that are open in style rather than ones that are dense and have filled-in areas.

Circles and curves. Use a freezer-paper circle and a walking foot to quilt circles or create a spiral that covers the entire quilt. Or, build an overall design of stitched curves in an organic way that complements your quilt top. Or, simply follow the outline of curved appliqué shapes to echo their design.

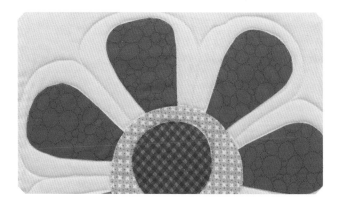

More about Quilting

You can learn more about my quilting techniques in my book *Pat Sloan's Teach Me to Machine Quilt* (Martingale, 2016).

Adding a Label

Creating a label for your quilt is an important part of the quiltmaking process. I like to use a triangle-shaped label because I can sew two of the sides of the label in the corner of my quilt before I attach the binding.

Follow these steps to make a triangle label.

1. **Cut a 6" square of muslin** or light-colored solid fabric. If you have a lot of information to write on the label, cut an 8" square. Cut the square in half diagonally to make two triangles. Set one triangle aside for another label.

2. **Using a Pigma pen,** write the desired information on the muslin triangle. Make sure to leave at least ¼" on all sides for the seam allowance.

3. **From a contrasting fabric,** (it's nice to use the binding fabric), cut a 1½" × 12" strip for a 6" square or a 1½" × 14" strip for an 8" square.

4. **Fold one long raw edge under ¼"** to the wrong side of the strip. Sew the strip to the long side of the triangle. Press the seam allowances toward the strip.

5. **On the back of the quilt,** pin the triangle onto the lower-right corner. Trim the edges of the strip even with the edges of the quilt.

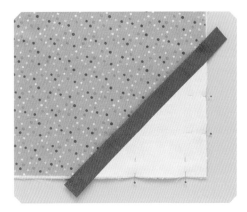

6. **Attach the binding** (see "Binding by Machine" on page 35). Once the binding is stitched, slip-stitch the diagonal edge of the label to the backing to secure the label.

What should you write on the label? Whatever you want to include! Your name as the quiltmaker is the minimum, but imagine future generations and what they'll want to know about your quilt.

- The name of the quilt and/or the pattern you used.

- Your full name as the maker (I'd use Pat Sloan, rather than Auntie Pat, for clarity).

- The year and month the quilt was completed.

- Who you're giving the quilt to and the reason, such as "Made with love for Katie Sloan for her 5th Birthday."

- The city and state or country where the quilt was made.

If you're shipping the quilt, I also highly recommend pinning a note to the quilt with your email and phone number. Then if the box is damaged, the shipping company will know who to contact.

Binding by Machine

When it comes to binding quilts, my preferred method is to attach the binding entirely by machine. It's fast, it's sturdy, and I save my hand-sewing time for other tasks.

PREPARING THE BINDING

For this projects in this book, I used a double-fold binding to finish the quilt edges. I always use a double-fold binding for quilts that will be washed since the stitching is secure.

1. Cut the number of 2¼"-wide strips from the binding fabric as indicated in the project instructions. The amount specified is enough to go around the perimeter of the quilt plus approximately 10" extra for joining strips and mitering corners.

2. Join the binding strips with a diagonal seam to make one long strip. Make sure the stitching goes from point to point where the two strips intersect.

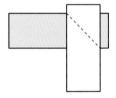

3. Trim the excess fabric and then press the seam allowances open.

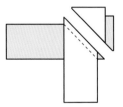

4. Press the binding strip in half lengthwise, wrong sides together and with raw edges aligned.

SEWING THE BINDING
TO THE QUILT BACK

I start by sewing the binding to the *back* of the quilt. Then I turn the binding to the front of the quilt and finish machine stitching it in place. That's right, you're going to sew the binding to the *back* of the quilt! Use a walking foot to make sure the quilt layers don't shift while you're stitching.

1. **Starting at the center of one side,** position the binding strip on one side of the back of the quilt, aligning the raw edges; pin the first edge in place.

2. **Using a straight stitch** and a ¼" seam allowance, begin sewing about 6" from the end of the binding and stop sewing ¼" from the corner; backstitch. Clip the thread and remove the quilt from under the presser foot.

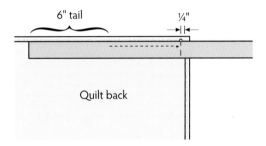

3. Fold the binding tail up at a 90° angle.

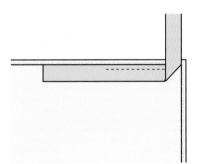

4. **Then bring the binding back down** onto itself to square the corner and align with the next side. Starting at the top edge, sew until you're ¼" from the next corner. Repeat the folding and stitching process at each corner.

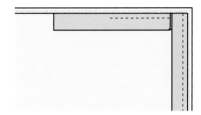

5. **When you are about 6"** from your starting point, stop sewing and backstitch. Clip the thread and remove the quilt from under the presser foot.

6. **Unfold the ends** of the binding strip. Fold one end up to create a 45° angle and the other end down to create a 45° angle so that the angled folds meet. Press the folds. With right sides together, align the folds; pin. Stitch on the fold line, backstitching at both ends. Trim the excess binding strip, leaving a ¼" seam allowance. Press the seam allowances open. Refold the binding and finish stitching it in place.

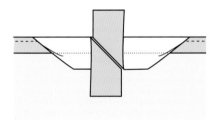

Hand Binding

If you prefer to sew the binding by hand, in step 1 sew the binding to the *front* of the quilt instead of the quilt back. Then follow the instructions in steps 2–6 to attach the binding. Once the binding is attached, fold the binding to the back of the quilt, covering the raw edges, and hand stitch it in place, mitering the corners as shown in step 4 on page 37.

FINISHING THE BINDING ON THE QUILT FRONT

To finish the binding by machine, turn your quilt over to the right side and fold the binding over to the front. Keep your walking foot on for this part as well.

1. **Set the straight stitch length** on your machine to 2.8.

2. **With the front facing up,** place one side of the quilt under the machine needle. Pull the binding from the back to the front, aligning the turned-under edge with the stitching line you made while attaching the binding to the back. The goal is to stitch about ⅛" from the fold on the binding. That way, the straight stitch on the back will be right next to the binding seam.

3. **Begin stitching.** Work slowly, folding the binding over the stitching line as you go. It's helpful to use a stiletto or seam ripper to help hold the fold in place.

4. **When you reach the corner,** fold the binding in as you've been doing, all the way to the outer corner. Then, without turning the quilt, fold the binding along the next edge over to meet the stitching line. This will form a mitered corner. Stitch right up to the corner and try to catch the fold of the miter.

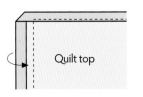
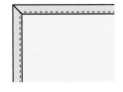

Quilt top

5. **Turn the quilt and continue stitching** along the next side of the quilt. Repeat until you've stitched along all four sides of the quilt.

6. **Hand stitch the miters closed** at each corner, on both the front and back of the quilt.

Caring for Your Quilt

Most of today's quilt fabrics resist bleeding and shrinkage very well, but it's still a great idea to prewash your fabric if you plan on washing the finished quilt (see "Prewashing Fabric" on page 12). If you want to wash your quilt, I recommend the following method.

♦ Machine wash your quilt in cool/tepid water using a mild detergent. Orvis, Dreft, and Ivory are mild laundry soaps that are good for washing 100% cotton quilts. Use just a little bit of detergent and do not use bleach.

♦ If the fabric has not been washed prior to making the quilt, use a dye-catcher sheet in the washer when washing your quilt for the first time. Dark colors like red, navy, green, and black may release excess dye, even after being prewashed. For safety, use a dye catcher sheet when washing a quilt with dark colors.

♦ Use the gentle or delicate cycle on your washing machine. Remove the quilt as soon as the cycle is finished.

♦ Check the quilt to see if any of the fabrics have bled. If there's any bleeding, don't put the quilt in the dryer. Keep rinsing with cool water until the bleeding stops. There are products at your local quilt shop, such as Retayne, to help if the bleeding is intense.

♦ Dry the quilt in the dryer at a low temperature setting. Do not overdry or you may set in wrinkles.

Block 1: Four Patch

FINISHED BLOCK SIZE: 12" × 12"

Block Specs

A Four Patch block is composed of four squares that are the same size. You'll use the same layout anytime four same-sized units are joined to make a block, such as the Rail Fence block (page 39). Practice sewing an accurate ¼" seam allowance so that the block measures 12½" square, including the seam allowances on the outer edges. You can use two matching light squares and two matching dark squares to make the block, like I did, or use four different fabrics for a scrappy block.

Materials

7" × 14" rectangle of light print (fabric A)

7" × 14" rectangle of dark print (fabric B)

Cutting

From the light print (fabric A), cut:
2 squares, 6½" × 6½"

From the dark print (fabric B), cut:
2 squares, 6½" × 6½"

Assembling the Block

Refer to "Sewing and Pressing" (page 17) as needed throughout.

1. **Lay the A and B squares** in two rows, alternating the dark and light squares in each row as shown.

2. **With right sides together,** join the squares into two rows. Press the seam allowances toward the B squares.

3. **Pin the rows right sides together,** nestling the center seams so that the top seamline is against the bottom seamline.

4. **Sew the rows together** to complete the Four Patch block. Press the seam allowances in one direction. The block should measure 12½" square, including the seam allowances. To make a table runner using the Four Patch block, see page 65.

Block 2: Rail Fence

--------✂<-------

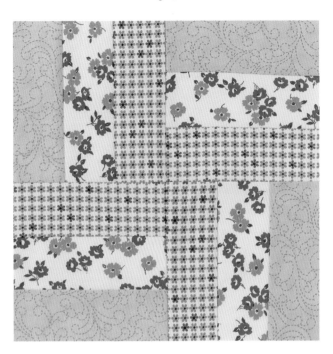

FINISHED BLOCK SIZE: 12" × 12"

Block Specs

With this block, you'll practice following your seam guideline to produce an accurate ¼" seam allowance. The Rail Fence block contains four identical units. Each unit is made of three strips of fabric and each unit measures 6½" square, including seam allowances. The top-left and bottom-right units are oriented vertically, and the other two units are rotated so the strips are horizontal. The block should measure 12½" square, including seam allowances. Try using one light, one medium, and one dark print, or use one light and two medium prints to make the block.

Materials

Yardage is based on 42"-wide fabric.

 ⅛ yard of dark print (fabric A)

 ⅛ yard of medium print (fabric B)

 ⅛ yard of light print (fabric C)

Cutting

From the dark print (fabric A), cut:
4 rectangles, 2½" × 6½"

From the medium print (fabric B), cut:
4 rectangles, 2½" × 6½"

From the light print (fabric C), cut:
4 rectangles, 2½" × 6½"

Making the Units

Refer to "Sewing and Pressing" (page 17) as needed throughout.

1. Lay out one fabric A, one fabric B, and one fabric C rectangle, placing the fabric B rectangle in the center.

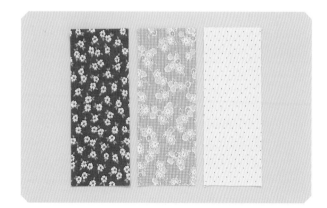

2. Place the A and B rectangles right sides together with raw edges aligned. Sew along one long edge using a ¼" seam allowance. Flip the rectangles open and press the seam allowances toward fabric B.

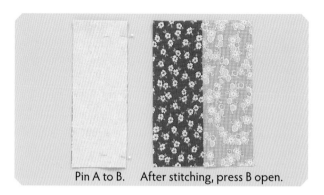

Pin A to B.   After stitching, press B open.

3. Place the C rectangle on top of the B rectangle, right sides together and raw edges aligned. Sew the rectangles together to complete the unit. Press the seam allowances toward fabric B. The unit should measure 6½" square, including seam allowances.

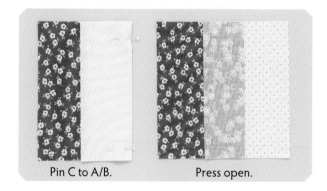

Pin C to A/B.   Press open.

4. Repeat steps 2 and 3 to make three more units. You should have a total of four identical units.

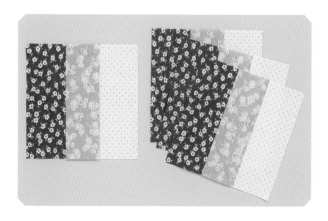

Assembling the Block

1. Lay out the four units as shown, with two oriented horizontally and two vertically. Fabric A is always toward the outside edge of the block.

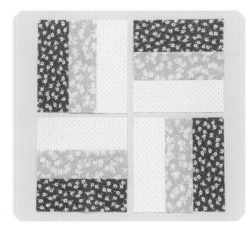

2. With right sides together, join the units into two rows.

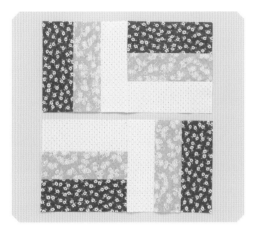

3. Press the seam allowances toward the C rectangles.

4. Pin the rows right sides together, nestling the center seams so that the top seamline is against the bottom seamline.

5. Sew the rows together to make the block. Press the seam allowances in one direction. The block should measure 12½" square. To make a quilt using the Rail Fence block, see page 68.

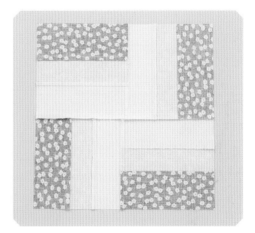

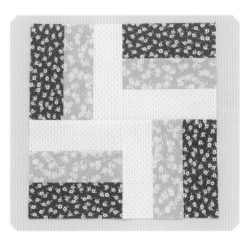

Block 3: Quarter Log Cabin

---✂---

FINISHED BLOCK SIZE: 12" × 12"

Block Specs

With this easy block, you'll work on keeping the block square as you build it. Using an accurate ¼" seam allowance is important as you sew rectangles to two sides of a square. The completed block should measure 12½" square, including the seam allowances on the outer edges. You'll need four fabrics for this blocks—three fabrics for the logs and one for the square.

Materials

 7" × 7" square of dark floral (fabric A)

 3" × 18" strip of medium print (fabric B)

 3" × 20" strip of light-medium print (fabric C)

 3" × 22" strip of light floral (fabric D)

Cutting

From the navy floral (fabric A), cut:
1 square, 6½" × 6½"

From the red print (fabric B), cut:
1 rectangle, 2½" × 6½"
1 rectangle, 2½" × 10½"

From the blue print (fabric C), cut:
1 rectangle, 2½" × 8½"
1 rectangle, 2½" × 10½"

From the blue floral (fabric D), cut:
1 rectangle, 2½" × 8½"
1 rectangle, 2½" × 12½"

Assembling the Block

Refer to "Sewing and Pressing" (page 17) as needed throughout. After sewing each seam, press the seam allowances toward each newly added rectangle.

1. Sew the 2½" × 6½" fabric B rectangle to the 6½" fabric A square, right sides together. The unit should measure 6½" × 8½", including seam allowances.

2. Sew the 2½" × 8½" fabric C rectangle to an adjacent side of the fabric A square, right sides together. The unit should measure 8½" square, including seam allowances.

3. Sew the 2½" × 8½" fabric D rectangle to the fabric B side of the unit from step 2, right sides together. The unit should measure 8½" × 10½", including seam allowances.

4. Sew the 2½" × 10½" fabric B rectangle to the fabric C side of the unit from step 3, right sides together. The unit should measure 10½" × 10½", including seam allowances.

5. Sew the 2½" × 10½" fabric C rectangle to unit from step 4 as shown. The unit should measure 10½" × 12½", including seam allowances.

6. Sew the 2½" × 12½" fabric D rectangle to unit from step 5 as shown to complete the Quarter Log Cabin block. The block should measure 12½" square, including seam allowances. To make a crib quilt or table mat using the Quarter Log Cabin block, see page 71.

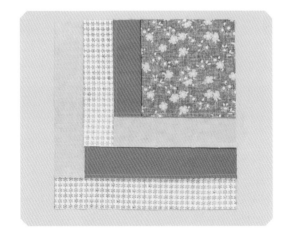

Block 4: Nine Patch

------ ✂ ------

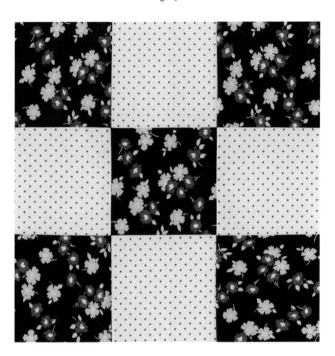

FINISHED BLOCK SIZE: 12" × 12"

Block Specs

A Nine Patch block has multiple seams that need to match within one block. You can use one light and one dark fabric to make this block, like I did, or you can use a third fabric for the center square. You can also make a scrappy block by using a variety of light and dark prints.

This is also a block layout you'll use again and again. In its basic form, nine individual squares are joined to make the block. In quiltmaking, many blocks are composed of nine same-sized pieced units, such as a Friendship Star block (page 78) and a Churn Dash block (page 82).

Materials

☐ 5" × 24" strip of dark print (fabric A)

☐ 5" × 20" strip of light print (fabric B)

Cutting

From the dark print (fabric A), cut:
5 squares, 4½" × 4½"

From the light print (fabric B), cut:
4 squares, 4½" × 4½"

Assembling the Block

Refer to "Sewing and Pressing" (page 17) as needed throughout.

1. Lay the fabric A and B squares in three rows, alternating the A and B squares in each row and from row to row as shown.

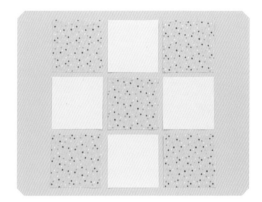

2. Sew a fabric A square to a fabric B square, right sides together, to make a two-square unit. Make three units.

3. **Press the seam allowances** toward the dark squares. Each unit should measure 4½" × 8½", including seam allowances. After pressing, make sure to return the unit to its correct position in the block layout.

4. **Add the remaining square** in each row. The top and bottom rows should begin and end with a fabric A square. The center row should begin and end with a fabric B square. Press the seam allowances toward the dark squares. Each row should measure 4½" × 12½", including seam allowances.

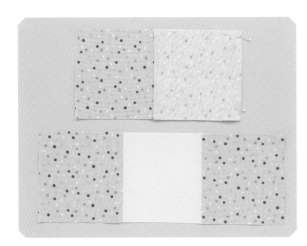

5. **Pin two rows right sides together,** nestling the seam intersections so that the top seamline is against the bottom seamline.

6. **Sew the rows together** and press the seam allowances toward the top row.

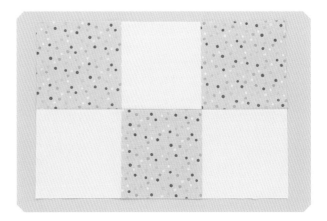

7. **Sew the bottom row** to the opposite side of the center row to complete the Nine Patch block. Press the seam allowances toward the bottom row. The block should measure 12½" square, including seam allowances. To make a quilt using the Nine Patch block, see page 74.

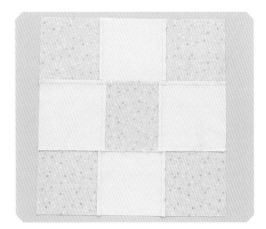

Block 5: Friendship Star

FINISHED BLOCK SIZE: 12" × 12"

Block Specs

The classic Friendship Star block is composed of a new shape—a triangle square! A triangle square is also known as a half-square-triangle unit. I use a method to make two at a time, which means the units are easy and almost foolproof. This is a wonderful technique to learn right from the start because you'll use it in many quilt patterns. A Friendship Star block requires four identical half-square-triangle units and four plain squares. You can use one light and one dark fabric to make a block, like I did, or you can use a third fabric for the center square.

Materials

Yardage is based on 42"-wide fabric.

☐ 6" × 42" strip of light print (fabric A)

▨ 6" × 18" strip of dark print (fabric B)

Cutting

From the light print (fabric A), cut:
2 squares, 5" × 5"
4 squares, 4½" × 4½"

From the dark print (fabric B), cut:
2 squares, 5" × 5"
1 square, 4½" × 4½"

Making the Half-Square-Triangle Units

Refer to "Sewing and Pressing" (page 17) as needed throughout.

1. Draw a diagonal line from corner to corner on the wrong side of both 5" fabric A squares.

Mark the Seamlines

You can mark the seamlines by drawing lines ¼" from both sides of the centerline.

2. **Place each marked square** on a 5" fabric B square, right sides together and edges aligned.

3. **Stitch ¼" from both sides** of the drawn line. Each stitched line will be the diagonal seamline of a half-square-triangle unit once the squares are cut apart.

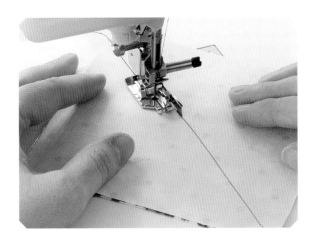

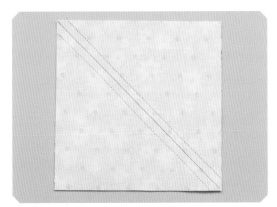

4. **Cut the squares apart** on the marked line to make two half-square-triangle units.

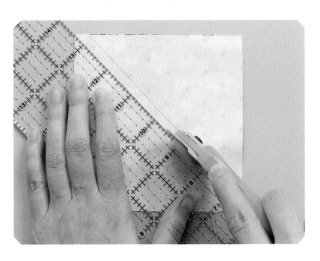

5. **Press the seam allowances** toward the darker triangle (fabric B). Make a total of four half-square-triangle units.

6. **The half-square-triangle units** are slightly oversized. Using a square ruler, place the diagonal line of the ruler on top of the seamline. Use a rotary cutter to trim a small amount from the first two sides of the unit.

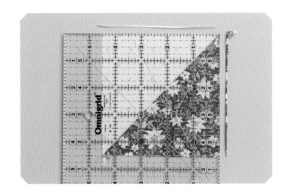

7. Turn the unit around and trim the other two sides so that the unit measures exactly 4½" square. In the same way, trim the remaining three units. When you use this method to trim the units, they are always the perfect size. You also remove the little triangles (also called dog ears) that stick out at the corners, which makes sewing the block together easier.

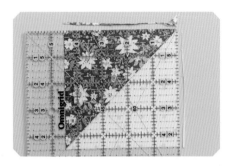

Half-Square-Triangle Unit Formula

There's an easy formula for making two half-square-triangle units at one time, which is the desired *finished* size of the unit plus 1" for seam allowances. For this block, the finished size of the half-square-triangle unit is 4". To make two half-square-triangle units, you need a 5" square (4" + 1" = 5") of each print.

Assembling the Block

Refer to "Sewing and Pressing" (page 17) as needed throughout. The construction of the Friendship Star block is similar to the Nine Patch block (page 44). The difference is that the half-square-triangle units have a seam at the corner, which means more layers of fabric to deal with. You may need to use the tip of a sewing stiletto to help guide the thicker end of the unit under your presser foot.

1. Lay out the half-square-triangle units, four 4½" fabric A squares, and the 4½" fabric B square in three rows, rotating the half-square-triangle units as shown. Check to make sure all of the triangles are positioned correctly. It's easy to rotate them incorrectly!

2. With right sides together, join the first two pieces in each row. Make three units. Press the seam allowances toward the squares. Each two-piece unit should measure 4½" × 8½", including seam allowances. After pressing, return the unit to its correct position in the block layout.

3. **Add the remaining square** or half-square-triangle unit in each row. The top and bottom rows should begin and end with an A square. The center row should begin and end with a half-square-triangle unit. Press the seam allowances toward the squares. Each row should measure 4½" × 12½", including seam allowances.

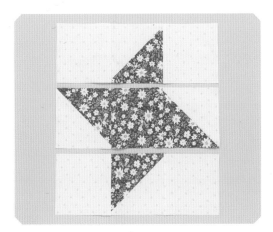

4. **Pin two rows right sides together,** nestling the seam intersections so that the top seamline is against the bottom seamline.

5. **Sew the rows together** and press the seam allowances toward the top row.

Perfect Points

Admittedly, it can be tricky to make nice points where seamlines come together at the same spot. For the best results, stitch a ¼" seam, making sure your seamline is just shy of the stitched X intersection. Open up the seam and see how it looks. If needed, you can sew the seam again with a slightly wider seam allowance. That's much easier than having to rip out one that's too wide to begin with.

6. **Sew the bottom row** to the opposite side of the center row to complete the Friendship Star block. Press the seam allowances toward the bottom row. The block should measure 12½" square, including seam allowances. To make a baby or wall quilt using the Friendship Star block, see page 78.

Block 6: Churn Dash

------- ✂ -------

FINISHED BLOCK SIZE: 12" × 12"

Block Specs

The Churn Dash is my all-time favorite block. It's composed of nine sections—half-square-triangle units, a pieced rectangle unit (I call it a rail unit), and a center square. With this block, you'll learn how to keep track of three different components to make one final block. And the units can easily be switched up by rotating them to create a whole new design. I used one light and one dark fabric to make the block, but you can use a third fabric in the rail unit if desired.

Materials

Yardage is based on 42"-wide fabric.

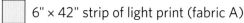 6" × 42" strip of light print (fabric A)

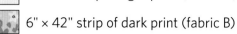 6" × 42" strip of dark print (fabric B)

Cutting

From the light print (fabric A), cut:
2 squares, 5" × 5"
1 square, 4½" × 4½"
4 rectangles, 2½" × 4½"

From the dark print (fabric B), cut:
2 squares, 5" × 5"
4 rectangles, 2½" × 4½"

Making the Rail Units

These units are similar to Rail Fence units, except they're composed of only two rectangles instead of three. It's easy to chain piece these units! Refer to "Sewing and Pressing" (page 17) as needed throughout.

1. Place a 2½" × 4½" fabric A rectangle on top of a fabric B rectangle, right sides together and edges aligned.

2. Sew the rectangles together along one long edge to make a rail unit. Press the seam allowances toward the fabric B rectangle. The unit should measure 4½" square, including seam allowances. Make four units.

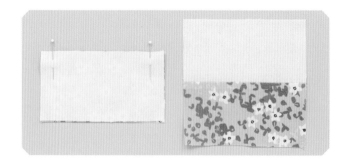

Making the Half-Square-Triangle Units

For detailed instructions and photos, see "Making the Half-Square-Triangle Units" (page 46).

1. **Draw a diagonal line** from corner to corner on the wrong side of each 5" fabric A square. Place each marked square on a 5" fabric B square, right sides together and edges aligned.

2. **Stitch ¼" from each side** of the drawn line. Cut the squares apart on the marked line to make two half-square-triangle units. Press the seam allowances toward the darker triangle. Make a total of four half-square-triangle units.

3. **The half-square-triangle units** are slightly oversized. Using a square ruler, trim each unit to measure 4½" square, including seam allowances.

Assembling the Block

1. **Lay out the half-square-triangle units**, rail units, and the fabric A 4½" square in three rows.

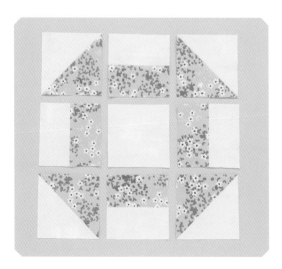

Nine Patch Arrangement

Let's take a closer look at block construction. Every nine-patch arrangement requires nine sections or patches, which are arranged in three rows of three units or squares.

- A Nine Patch block (page 44) is constructed of nine squares.

- A Friendship Star block (page 46) is composed of four half-square-triangle units and five squares.

- A Churn Dash block requires four half-square-triangle units, four rail units, and one center square.

As you look at quilt blocks, you'll find lots of variations on what makes up each of the nine patches in this block style. Knowing the style of a block helps you break down the block into manageable sections.

2. **With right sides together,** join the first two pieces in each row to make a two-piece unit. Make three units. Press the seam allowances toward the rail units. Each two-piece unit should measure 4½" × 8½", including seam allowances. After pressing, make sure to return the unit to its correct position in the block layout.

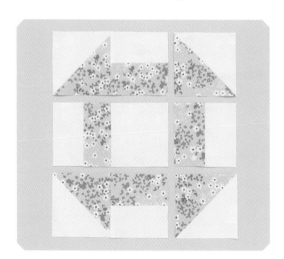

3. Add the remaining half-square-triangle unit or rail unit in each row. The top and bottom rows should begin and end with a half-square-triangle unit. The center row should begin and end with a rail unit. Press the seam allowances toward the squares. Each row should measure 4½" × 12½", including seam allowances.

4. **Pin two rows right sides together,** nestling the seam intersections so that the top seamline is against the bottom seamline.

5. **Sew the rows together** and press the seam allowances toward the center row.

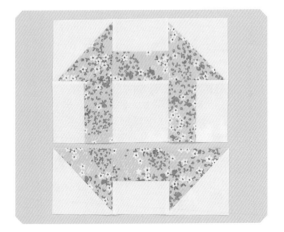

6. **Sew the bottom row** to the opposite side of the center row to complete the Churn Dash block. Press the seam allowances toward the center row. The block should measure 12½" square, including seam allowances. To make a table topper using the Churn Dash block, see page 82.

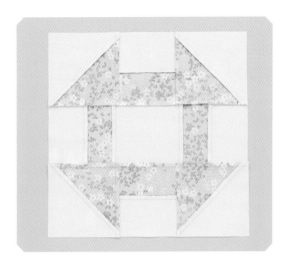

Block 7: Sawtooth Star

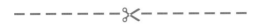

FINISHED BLOCK SIZE: 12" × 12"

Block Specs

The star-point units in this block are made using the very handy stitch-and-flip method. For this technique, squares are stitched to the corners of rectangles along the diagonal. The squares are then flipped open to form triangles. Lots of quilt blocks use this basic method to create different units. The structure of this block is also new in our sequence of learning. The block still has nine sections, but the sections are not all the same size. I used three different fabrics to make a block. Another option would be to use the same fabric for the star points and center square and a different one for the background fabric.

Materials

Yardage is based on 42"-wide fabric.

 4" × 42" strip of light print (fabric A)

 4" × 42" strip of red solid (fabric B)

 7" × 7" strip of dark print (fabric C)

Cutting

From the light print (fabric A), cut:
4 squares, 3½" × 3½"
4 rectangles, 3½" × 6½"

From the red solid (fabric B), cut:
8 squares, 3½" × 3½"

From the dark print (fabric C), cut:
1 square, 6½" × 6½"

Making the Flying-Geese Units

I use the stitch-and-flip method to make the star-point units. While you could use two half-square-triangle units, you would need to sew the units together, which means you'd have a seam in the center of the star-point unit. With the stitch-and-flip method, you'll save time and you won't have a center seam in the unit. Refer to "Sewing and Pressing" (page 17) as needed throughout.

1. Draw a diagonal line from corner to corner on the wrong side of each 3½" fabric B square.

2. Pin a marked square on one end of a 3½" × 6½" fabric A rectangle, right sides together and raw edges aligned. Sew along the line, one thin thread's width from the line, on what will be the seam-allowance side of the line.

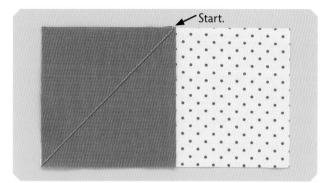

Stitching Tips

Here are a few tips for accurately sewing the squares to the rectangle.

- Start sewing at the corner of the square that is on the inside of the rectangle, not at the outer corner. I find I'm more accurate if I start sewing with more fabric underneath the square than starting at the point.

- Sew slowly and follow the line accurately; this will be your seamline.

- Sew *along* the line, one thin thread's width from the line, on what will be the seam-allowance side of the line. The stitched line takes up a little bit of space. By stitching along the line, you won't lose any fabric when you fold the triangle over the seam allowances and press.

3. Flip the square back over the corner with the right side facing up and press, being careful not to stretch the square. The seam allowances will automatically be pressed toward the triangle. Check the unit for accuracy. See "Check Before Trimming" below.

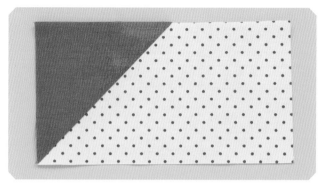

Check Before Trimming

Before trimming the excess corner fabric, I flip the square back over the corner with the right side facing up and check it for accuracy. The edges of the triangle should lie exactly on the corner of the rectangle, with all three layers of fabric aligned in the corner. If the edges don't match, resew the seam.

4. Unfold the fabric B square and place the ¼" line of a ruler on the stitched line.

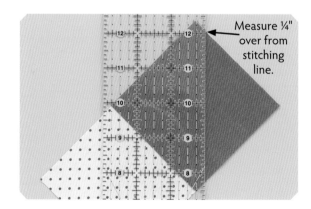

Measure ¼" over from stitching line.

5. Trim away the excess corner fabric, leaving a ¼" seam allowance. Trimming the excess fabric will reduce the bulk in the corners of the unit. Re-press the resulting triangle open.

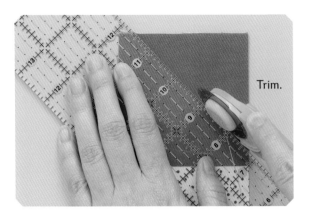

Trim.

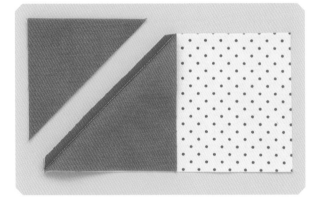

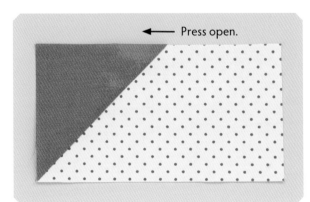

Press open.

6. Place a second marked square on the other end of the rectangle, right sides together and raw edges aligned. Sew and press, and then trim away the excess corner fabric in the same way as before. Make a total of four star-point units. Each unit should measure 3½" × 6½", including seam allowances.

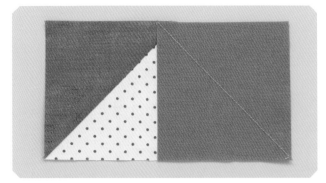

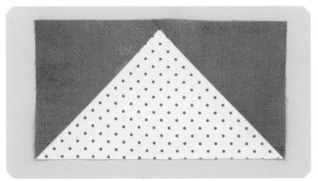

Trimmed Triangles

What do you do with the triangles that are trimmed from the star-point units? Sew the triangles together along their long edges to make bonus half-square-triangle units. Following the instructions and photos (page 47), trim the units to measure 2½" square and set them aside for another project.

Assembling the Block

Refer to "Sewing and Pressing" (page 17) as needed throughout.

1. Lay out the four star-point units, the four 3½" fabric A squares, and the 6½" fabric C square in three rows, making sure to rotate the star-point units as shown.

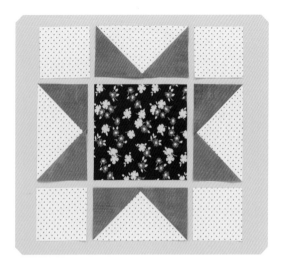

2. For the top row, sew a fabric A square to each end of a star-point unit. Press the seam allowances toward the fabric A squares. The row should measure 3½" × 12½", including seam allowances. Repeat to make the bottom row.

3. For the middle row, sew a star-point unit to opposite sides of the fabric C square. Press the seam allowances toward the fabric C square. The row should measure 6½" × 12½", including seam allowances.

4. Pin the top and middle rows right sides together, nestling the seam intersections so that the top seamline is against the bottom seamline. Sew the rows together and press the seam allowances toward the middle row.

5. Sew the bottom row to the opposite side of the middle row to complete the Sawtooth Star block. The block should measure 12½" square, including seam allowances. To make a table topper using the Sawtooth Star block, see page 86.

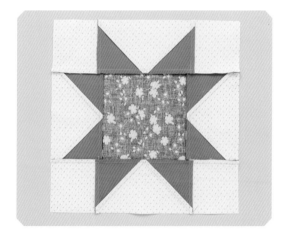

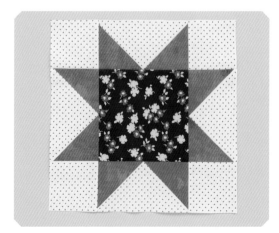

Block 8:
Hip to Be Square

------- ✂ -------

FINISHED BLOCK SIZE: 12" × 12"

Block Specs

The next technique you'll learn is fusible machine appliqué. Appliqué is a very forgiving form of quiltmaking—you can make any shape and place it where you want to. My technique is easy and fun, and the appliqué is nice and soft. For this block, we'll start with a geometric shape in two sizes and move on to an appliquéd flower in the next block. That way you'll have a chance to try different shapes. Appliqué can be combined with patchwork, but it's better to start with a plain background so the design isn't too busy. With this square you can showcase a beautiful piece of fabric and accent it with companion prints.

Materials

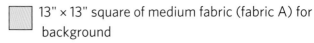 13" × 13" square of medium fabric (fabric A) for background

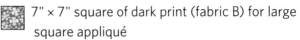 7" × 7" square of dark print (fabric B) for large square appliqué

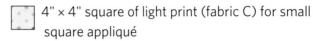 4" × 4" square of light print (fabric C) for small square appliqué

7" × 7" square of paper-backed fusible web

Preparing the Appliqués

Refer to "Easy Fusible Appliqué" (page 25) as needed throughout.

1. Using a pencil and either a square ruler or a long ruler, trace each square pattern (page 60) onto the fusible web.

2. Roughly cut out the large outer square, leaving ½" beyond the drawn line. Cut through the excess web around the square, through the marked line, and into the interior of the outer square. Then cut away the excess fusible web on

the *inside* of the larger square, leaving less than ¼" inside the drawn line. In the same way, prepare the small square for appliqué.

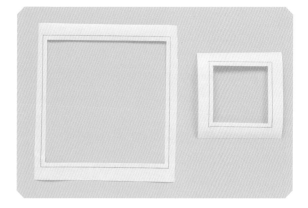

3. Position the small fusible-web square on the wrong side of the fabric C square. Place the large fusible-web square on the wrong side of the fabric B square. Fuse as instructed by the manufacturer.

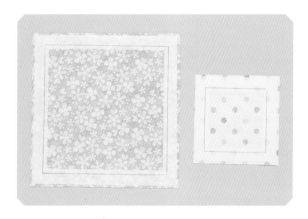

4. Using a ruler and rotary cutter, cut out each square on the marked lines. Remove the paper backing from each square.

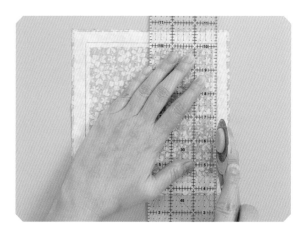

Stitching the Block

Refer to "Easy Fusible Appliqué" (page 25) as needed throughout.

1. Place the 13" fabric A background square on your ironing board, right side up. Position the prepared fabric B square in the upper-right section of the background square. Make sure the fabric B square is at least ¾" from the outer edges of the fabric A square to allow for trimming the background square to size. Place the prepared fabric C square on top of the fabric B square.

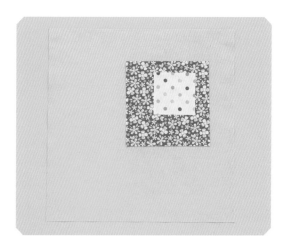

Arranging the Appliqués

I arranged my appliquéd squares in an asymmetrical setting instead of centering them in the middle of the background square. The beauty of appliqué is that it's easy to move things around before you adhere the shapes. Rearrange the squares until you're pleased with the placement.

2. Once you're pleased with the placement, fuse the squares in place. Stitch around the outer edges of each square using a matching or contrasting thread. I used a straight machine stitch for this step.

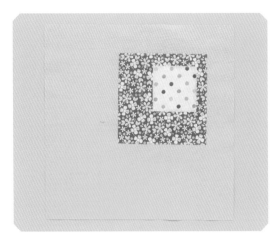

3. Referring to "Squaring Up Blocks" (page 23), trim the block to measure 12½" square, including the seam allowances. To make a table runner using the Hip to Be Square block, see page 90.

Sewing a Straight Stitch

Here are a few tips for sewing a straight stitch along the edge of each square.

- Start sewing along one side, not at a corner.

- Bring the bobbin thread to the top. Then hold the thread tails so they don't get pulled into the feed dogs on your machine.

- Stitch about ⅛" *inside* each square to secure it.

- When you get to the corner, stop, pivot, and continue along the next side.

- When you reach the starting point, stop and cut the thread, leaving a long tail.

- Pull the top and bobbin threads to the back. Tie a knot on the wrong side to secure the thread. I tie a knot on the back of the appliqué instead of backstitching, because it looks neater and smoother.

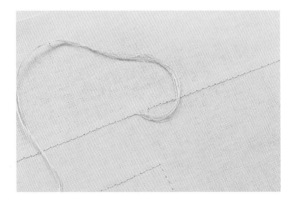

Knot the thread tails on the back of the block.

Patterns do not include
seam allowances.

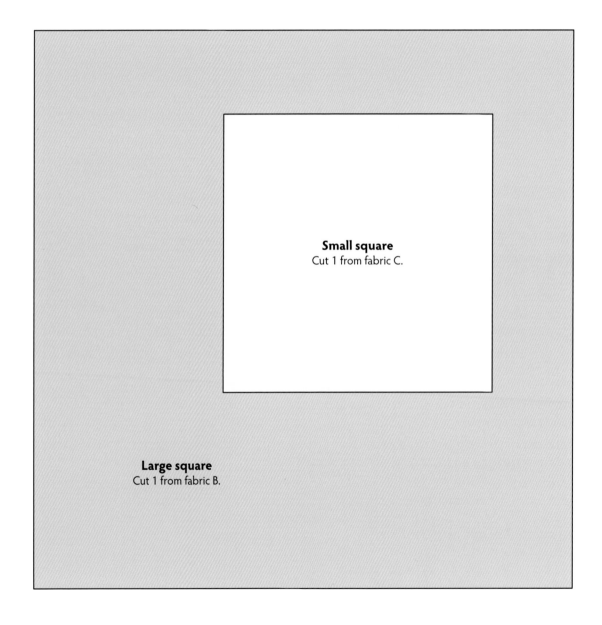

Small square
Cut 1 from fabric C.

Large square
Cut 1 from fabric B.

Block 9: Beautiful Bloom

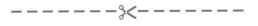

FINISHED BLOCK SIZE: 12" × 12"

Block Specs

Appliqué can make your quiltmaking come alive. You can create all kinds of shapes, but let's practice with a simple flower. The flower is composed of seven petals, a large circle, and a small circle. The ends of the petals are tucked under the large circle. In this lesson, you'll learn how to center and layer the shapes on a plain background square and how to appliqué curves.

Materials

 13" × 13" square of light print (fabric A) for background

 9" × 12" rectangle of dark print (fabric B) for petal appliqués

 6" × 6" square of medium print (fabric C) for large circle

 4" × 4" square of light-medium print (fabric D) for small circle

½ yard of paper-backed fusible web

Preparing the Appliqués

Refer to "Easy Fusible Appliqué" (page 25) as needed throughout.

1. **Using the patterns (page 64),** trace the number of shapes indicated on the patterns onto the fusible web. Roughly cut out each shape, leaving ½" beyond the drawn line. Cut through the excess web around the shape, through the marked line, and into the interior of the shape. Then cut away the excess fusible web on the *inside* of the shape, leaving less than ¼" inside the drawn line.

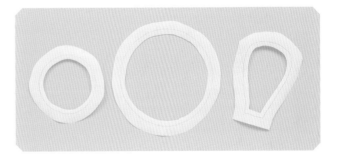

2. Position the fusible-web shapes on the wrong side of the fabrics indicated on the patterns. Fuse as instructed by the manufacturer.

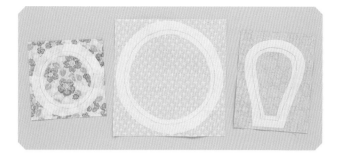

3. Cut out each prepared appliqué shape on the marked lines using scissors. Remove the paper backing from each shape.

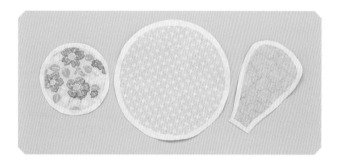

Stitching the Block

Refer to "Easy Fusible Appliqué" (page 25) as needed throughout.

1. Place the 13" fabric A background square on your ironing board, right side up. Fold the square in half and press a center vertical crease. Unfold the square. Refold the square in half and press a center horizontal crease. The creased lines are your guidelines for centering the appliqués.

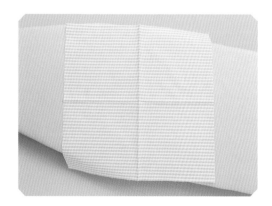

2. Fold the prepared fabric C circle in half vertically and horizontally, right sides together, to make a quarter circle. Place the folded circle on top of the background square and align the folds with the center creases on the square. The circle should be perfectly centered.

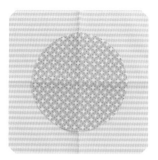

3. Place the fabric D circle on top of the fabric C circle. I purposefully placed mine off center to add interest.

4. Evenly space the fabric B petals around the fabric C circle, tucking the end of each petal under the circle. Make sure to place each petal at least ¾" in from the outer edge of the square to allow for trimming the background square and the seam allowances all around the edges of the square.

5. **Remove both circles** and fuse the petal appliqués in place. It's easier to stitch the petals and then add the circles after stitching. Using a straight stitch, sew around the outer edges of each petal using a matching or contrasting thread. See "Appliquéing the Petals and Circles" below right.

6. **Reposition the fabric C and D circles** in the center of the background square, making sure the ends of the petals are covered. Fuse in place. Using a straight stitch, sew around the outer edges of each circle using a matching or contrasting thread.

7. **Referring to "Squaring Up Blocks"** (page 23), trim the block to measure 12½" square, including the seam allowances. To make a table runner using the Beautiful Bloom block, see page 93.

Appliquéing the Petals and Circles

Here are a few tips for sewing a straight stitch around the edge of each petal.

- Start sewing at the base of the petal.

- Bring the bobbin thread to the top. Then hold onto the thread tails so they don't get pulled into the feed dogs on your machine.

- Stitch about ⅛" inside each petal to secure it.

- Slowly stitch around the curve, stopping with the needle in the down position and pivoting the petal to maintain a consistent distance from the edge. Stop stitching when you reach the base of the petal. You don't need to secure the thread at the base of the petal because the stitching will be covered by the center circle.

- Stitch on the background to the next petal. Then stitch around the petal. Continue in the same manner until all seven petals are stitched.

- For the circles, pull the top and bobbin threads to the back. Tie a knot on the wrong side to secure the thread.

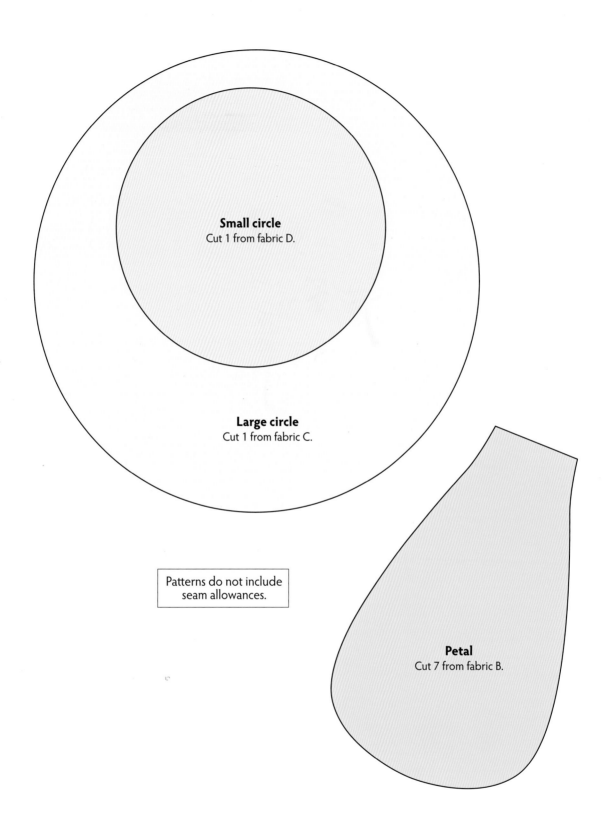

Small circle
Cut 1 from fabric D.

Large circle
Cut 1 from fabric C.

Patterns do not include
seam allowances.

Petal
Cut 7 from fabric B.

Four Patch Table Runner

FINISHED QUILT SIZE: 16½" × 40½"
FINISHED BLOCK SIZE: 12" × 12"

The Four Patch block is a wonderful way to show off your fabrics. When you join three blocks in a row you create a gorgeous table runner and you practice nesting your seams. With this project, you'll also learn to add border strips to the table runner.

Materials

Yardage is based on 42"-wide fabric.
¼ yard of light print (fabric A) for blocks
¼ yard of blue floral (fabric B) for blocks
⅝ yard of navy dot (fabric C) for border and binding
1⅜ yards of fabric for backing
21" × 45" piece of batting

Cutting

From the light print (fabric A), cut:
6 squares, 6½" × 6½"

From the blue floral (fabric B), cut:
6 squares, 6½" × 6½"

From the navy dot (fabric C), cut:
2 strips, 2½" × 36½"
2 strips, 2½" × 16½"
4 strips, 2¼" × 42"

Making the Blocks

Use a ¼" seam allowance throughout. After sewing each seam, press the seam allowances in the directions indicated by the arrows. For detailed instructions and photos, refer to "Block 1: Four Patch" (page 38).

1. Lay out two A and two B squares in two rows as shown.

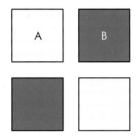

2. Sew the squares together into rows. Join the rows to complete a Four Patch block. Press. The block should measure 12½" square. Make a total of three blocks.

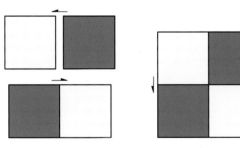

Make 3 blocks,
12½" x 12½".

Assembling the Table Runner

1. Join the blocks side by side to make a 12½" × 36½" row as shown in the table runner assembly diagram above right.

2. Refer to "Adding Borders" (page 29) as needed. Sew the 2½" × 36½" fabric C strips to the long sides of the runner top. Sew the 2½" × 16½" fabric C strips to the ends of the table runner to complete the border. The table runner should measure 16½" × 40½".

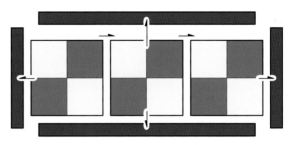

Table-runner assembly

Finishing the Table Runner

For more detailed information about any finishing steps, refer to "Finishing Your Quilt" (page 31).

1. Cut the backing fabric to make a backing approximately 4" longer and wider than the table runner.

2. Layer the table runner, batting, and backing; baste the layers together.

3. Quilt. The sample shown is machine quilted with evenly spaced straight lines along the length of the table runner. A straight line is quilted through the center of each border.

4. Make, sign, and date a label and attach it to the back of your table runner.

5. Join the fabric C 2¼"-wide strips end to end to make one long strip. Bind the quilt edges by hand or machine using the pieced strip.

Rail Fence Quilt

------ ✂ ------

FINISHED QUILT SIZE: 48½" × 60½"
FINISHED BLOCK SIZE: 12" × 12"

The Rail Fence is a fun quilt for working with different fabric choices. You can lay out the strips in different settings and different colors to see what you like best—all before you sew! As you work on this quilt, you'll become comfortable with sewing an accurate ¼" seam allowance.

Materials

Yardage is based on 42"-wide fabric.
40 strips, 2½" × 42", of assorted light, medium, and dark prints for blocks
½ yard of yellow dot (fabric D) for binding
3¼ yards of fabric for backing
55" × 67" piece of batting

Cutting

For each block, choose one light, one medium, and one dark print and label them fabric A, fabric B, and fabric C. Repeat the cutting instructions to make 20 blocks, keeping the fabrics for each block separate.

FOR ONE BLOCK

From fabric A, cut:
4 rectangles, 2½" × 6½"

From fabric B, cut:
4 rectangles, 2½" × 6½"

From fabric C, cut:
4 rectangles, 2½" × 6½"

FOR BINDING

From the yellow dot (fabric D), cut:
6 strips, 2¼" × 42"

Making the Blocks

For each block, use the rectangles from a fabric A, a fabric B, and a fabric C. Use a ¼" seam allowance throughout. After sewing each seam, press the seam allowances in the directions indicated by the arrows. For detailed instructions and photos, refer to "Block 2: Rail Fence" (page 39).

1. Join the fabric A, fabric B, and fabric C rectangles along their long edges to make a 6½" square unit, including seam allowances. Make four identical units.

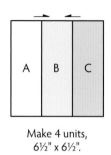

Make 4 units,
6½" x 6½".

2. Lay out the units from step 1 as shown. Sew the units together into rows. Join the rows to complete a Rail Fence block. The block should measure 12½" square, including seam allowances. Make a total of 20 blocks.

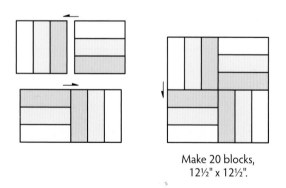

Make 20 blocks,
12½" x 12½".

Assembling the Quilt Top

Use a ¼" seam allowance throughout. After sewing each seam, press the seam allowances in the directions indicated by the arrows.

1. Lay out the blocks in five rows of four blocks each as shown in the quilt assembly diagram above right.

2. Sew the blocks together into rows. Join the blocks to complete the quilt top. The quilt top should measure 48½" × 60½", including seam allowances.

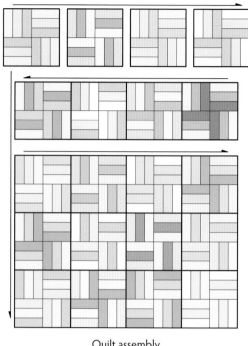

Quilt assembly

Finishing the Quilt Top

For more detailed information about any finishing steps, refer to "Finishing Your Quilt" (page 31).

1. Cut the backing fabric into two equal lengths and sew them together to make a backing approximately 6" longer and wider than the quilt top.

2. Layer the quilt top, batting, and backing; baste the layers together.

3. Quilt. The sample shown is machine quilted in an allover pattern of evenly spaced wavy lines, stitched parallel to the long edges of the quilt top.

4. Make, sign, and date a label and attach it to the back of your quilt.

5. Join the 2¼"-wide fabric D strips end to end to make one long strip. Bind the quilt edges by hand or machine using the pieced strip.

Quarter Log Cabin Quilt

--------- ✂ ---------

FINISHED QUILT SIZE: 24½" × 24½"
FINISHED BLOCK SIZE: 12" × 12"

Many quilters want to make a baby quilt as their first project. Four Quarter Log Cabin blocks sewn together make a nice crib-size quilt, wall quilt, or table mat. To create a beautiful lap quilt, make more blocks using a variety of fabrics or add borders to enlarge the quilt.

Materials

Yardage is based on 42"-wide fabric.
¼ yard of multicolored print (fabric A) for blocks
¼ yard of green print (fabric B) for blocks
⅜ yard of red floral (fabric C) for blocks
⅜ yard of orange print (fabric D) for blocks
⅜ yard of red print (fabric E) for binding
⅞ yard of fabric for backing
29" × 29" piece of batting

Cutting

From the multicolored print (fabric A), cut:
4 squares, 6½" × 6½"

From the green print (fabric B), cut:
2 strips, 2½" × 42"; crosscut into:
    4 strips, 2½" × 6½"
    4 strips, 2½" × 10½"

From the red floral (fabric C), cut:
3 strips, 2½" × 42"; crosscut into:
    4 strips, 2½" × 8½"
    4 strips, 2½" × 10½"

From the orange print (fabric D), cut:
3 strips, 2½" × 42"; crosscut into:
    4 strips, 2½" × 8½"
    4 strips, 2½" × 12½"

From the red print (fabric E), cut:
3 strips, 2¼" × 42"

Making the Blocks

Use a ¼" seam allowance throughout. After sewing each seam, press the seam allowances toward the newly added rectangle. For detailed instructions and photos, refer to "Block 3: Quarter Log Cabin" (page 42).

1. Sew a 2½" × 6½" fabric B rectangle to a 6½" fabric A square. The unit should measure 6½" × 8½", including seam allowances. Sew a

2½" × 8½" fabric C rectangle to an adjacent side of the fabric A square. The unit should now measure 8½" square, including seam allowances. Make four units.

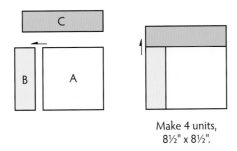

Make 4 units,
8½" x 8½".

2. Sew a 2½" × 8½" fabric D rectangle to a unit from step 1. Sew a 2½" × 10½" fabric B rectangle to the unit. The unit should measure 10½" × 10½", including seam allowances. Make four units.

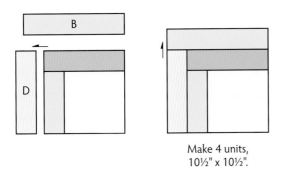

Make 4 units,
10½" x 10½".

3. Sew a 2½" × 10½" fabric C rectangle to a unit from step 2. Sew a 2½" × 12½" fabric D rectangle to the unit to complete a Quarter Log Cabin block. The block should measure 12½" square, including seam allowances. Make a total of four blocks.

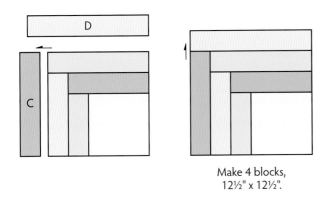

Make 4 blocks,
12½" x 12½".

Assembling the Quilt Top

Use a ¼" seam allowance throughout. After sewing each seam, press the seam allowances in the directions indicated by the arrows.

1. Lay out the blocks in two rows of two blocks each as shown in the quilt assembly diagram.

2. Sew the blocks together into rows. Join the blocks to complete the quilt top. The quilt top should measure 24½" square, including seam allowances.

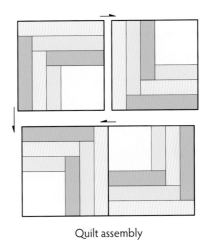

Quilt assembly

Finishing the Quilt Top

For more detailed information about any finishing steps, refer to "Finishing Your Quilt" (page 31).

1. Cut the backing fabric to make a backing approximately 4" longer and wider than the quilt top.

2. Layer the quilt top, batting, and backing; baste the layers together.

3. Quilt. On the sample quilt, a wavy line is machine quilted through the middle of each round of rectangles on each block. A wavy line is quilted diagonally through the center of the square.

4. Make, sign, and date a label and attach it to the back of your quilt.

5. Join the 2¼"-wide fabric E strips end to end to make one long strip. Bind the quilt edges by hand or machine using the pieced strip.

Nine Patch Quilt

✂

FINISHED QUILT SIZE: 48½" × 48½"
FINISHED BLOCK SIZE: 12" × 12"

For this project, you'll extend your skills to include sashing between the blocks, a cornerstone square where the sashing strips meet, and a border with corner squares. Not to worry—it's all strips and squares. This is a wonderful way to set your quilt blocks into a quilt. You'll find that you can use this setting for any type of block you make.

Materials

Yardage is based on 42"-wide fabric.
1 yard of green dot (fabric A) for blocks
¾ yard of white solid (fabric B) for blocks
½ yard of navy print (fabric C) for sashing and border corners
6" × 6" square of green solid (fabric D) for sashing cornerstones
1 yard of navy floral (fabric E) for border and binding
2½ yards of fabric for backing
53" × 53" piece of batting

Cutting

From the green dot (fabric A), cut:
6 strips, 4½" × 42"; crosscut into 45 squares, 4½" × 4½"

From the white solid (fabric B), cut:
5 strips, 4½" × 42"; crosscut into 36 squares, 4½" × 4½"

From the navy print (fabric C), cut:
4 strips, 2½" × 42"; crosscut into 12 strips, 2½" × 12½"
4 squares, 4½" × 4½"

From the green solid (fabric D), cut:
4 squares, 2½" × 2½"

From the navy floral (fabric E), cut:
4 strips, 4½" × 40½"
6 strips, 2¼" × 42"

From the backing fabric, cut:
1 rectangle, 40½" × 53"
1 strip, 13½" × 40½"
1 square, 13½" × 13½"

Making the Blocks

Use a ¼" seam allowance throughout. After sewing each seam, press the seam allowances in the directions indicated by the arrows. For detailed instructions and photos, refer to "Block 4: Nine Patch" (page 44).

1. Lay out five fabric A squares and four fabric B squares in three rows as shown.

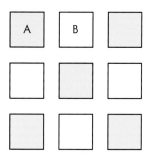

2. Sew the blocks together into rows. Join the rows to complete a Nine Patch block. The block should measure 12½" square, including seam allowances.

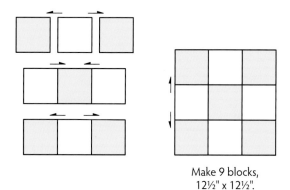

Make 9 blocks,
12½" x 12½".

Assembling the Quilt Top

1. Join three blocks and two fabric C 2½" × 12½" strips as shown to make a block row. The row should measure 12½" × 40½", including seam allowances. Make three rows.

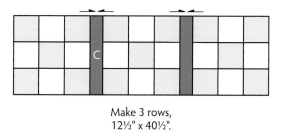

Make 3 rows,
12½" x 40½".

2. Join three 2½" × 12½" fabric C strips and two fabric D squares as shown to make a sashing row. The row should measure 2½" × 40½", including seam allowances. Make two rows.

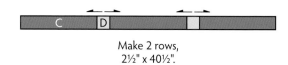

Make 2 rows,
2½" x 40½".

3. Join the block rows and sashing rows as shown in the quilt assembly diagram on page 77 to complete the quilt-top center, which should measure 40½" × 40½", including seam allowances.

4. Sew 4½" × 40½" fabric E strips to opposite sides of the quilt top. Sew 4½" fabric C squares to *both* ends of each remaining 4½" × 40½" fabric E strip. Sew the strips to the top and bottom of the quilt top as shown in the quilt assembly diagram.

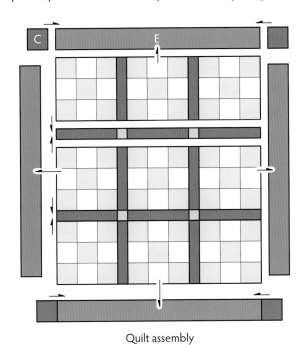

Quilt assembly

Finishing the Quilt Top

For more detailed information about any finishing steps, refer to "Finishing Your Quilt" (page 31).

1. **To make the backing,** sew the 13½" square to one end of the 13½" × 40½" strip to make a strip that's 13½" × 53". Sew the strip to the long side of

the 40½" × 53" rectangle to make a backing that measures 53" square.

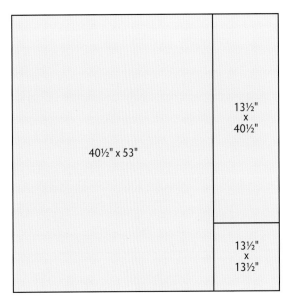

Make a 53" square backing.

2. **Layer the quilt top,** batting, and backing; baste the layers together.

3. **Quilt.** In the sample shown, diagonal lines are machine quilted through the blocks to create a large X. Wavy lines are quilted through the middle of the sashing strips and squares. Evenly spaced wavy lines are quilted in the border.

4. **Make, sign, and date a label** and attach it to the back of your quilt.

5. **Join the 2¼"-wide fabric E strips** end to end to make one long strip. Bind the quilt edges by hand or machine using the pieced strip.

Friendship Star Quilt

✂

FINISHED QUILT SIZE: 40½" × 40½"
FINISHED BLOCK SIZE: 12" × 12"

Making several Friendship Star blocks allows you to practice making half-square-triangle units, and by the end you'll be making them like a pro! For this quilt, we'll set the blocks side by side and you'll match the seam junctions from row to row. Add the optional appliqué to really make this quilt shine, or leave it off for a simple, classic look.

Materials

Yardage is based on 42"-wide fabric.

1½ yards of cream print (fabric A) for blocks and border

¾ yard of red print (fabric B) for blocks

½ yard of green print (fabric C) for binding and optional appliquéd circles

1¾ yards of fabric for backing

45" × 45" piece of batting

¼ yard of paper-backed fusible web (optional)

Cutting

From the cream print (fabric A), cut:

3 strips, 5" × 42"; crosscut into 18 squares, 5" × 5"

5 strips, 4½" × 42"; crosscut into 36 squares, 4½" × 4½"

2 strips, 2½" × 36½"

2 strips, 2½" × 40½"

From the red print (fabric B), cut:

3 strips, 5" × 42"; crosscut into 18 squares, 5" × 5"

2 strips, 4½" × 42"; crosscut into 9 squares, 4½" × 4½"

From the green print (fabric C), cut:

5 strips, 2¼" × 42"

Set aside the remainder of the fabric for the optional appliquéd circles.

From the backing fabric, cut:

1 rectangle, 40" × 45½"

1 strip, 6" × 40"

1 square, 6" × 6"

Making the Blocks

Use a ¼" seam allowance throughout. After sewing each seam, press the seam allowances in the directions indicated by the arrows. For detailed instructions and photos, refer to "Block 5: Friendship Star" (page 46).

1. **Draw a diagonal line** from corner to corner on the wrong side of each 5" fabric A square. Place a marked square on a 5" fabric B square, right sides together and raw edges aligned. Stitch ¼" from each side of the drawn line. Cut the squares apart on the marked line to make two half-square-triangle units. Press and trim the units to measure 4½" square. Make a total of 36 units.

Make 36 units, 4½" x 4½".

2. **Lay four half-square-triangle units,** four 4½" fabric A squares, and one 4½" fabric B square in three rows, rotating the half-square-triangle units as shown.

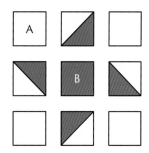

3. **Sew the pieces together into rows.** Join the rows to complete a Friendship Star block. The block should measure 12½" square, including seam allowances. Make a total of nine blocks.

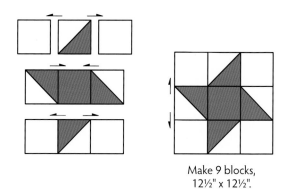

Make 9 blocks, 12½" x 12½".

Assembling the Quilt Top

1. **Lay out the blocks in three rows** of three blocks each as shown in the quilt assembly diagram below. Sew the blocks together into rows. Join the rows to complete the quilt-top center, which should measure 36½" square, including seam allowances.

2. **Sew the 2½" × 36½" fabric A strips** to opposite sides of the quilt top. Sew the 2½" × 40½" fabric A strips to the top and bottom to complete the border. The quilt top should measure 40½" square, including seam allowances.

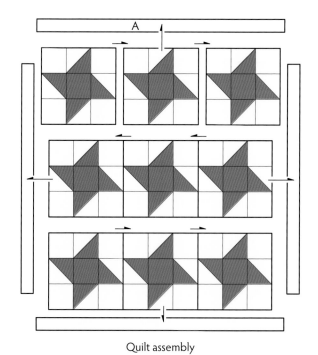

Quilt assembly

Adding the Appliquéd Dots

I added an appliquéd dot in the center of each block and on top of the seam intersections where the four blocks meet. The appliqué is optional but I thought it added a little pizzazz to the quilt.

1. Referring to "Easy Fusible Appliqué" and using the dot pattern at right, trace 13 dots onto the fusible web. Roughly cut out each shape, about ½" beyond the drawn line.

2. Position the fusible-web dots on the wrong side of fabric C. Fuse as instructed by the manufacturer. Cut out the dots on the marked lines. Remove the paper backing from each dot.

3. Place a dot in the center of each block. Center a dot atop the seam intersections as shown in the photo (page 78). Fuse the appliqués in place. Straight stitch around the outer edges of each dot using matching thread.

Finishing the Quilt Top

For more detailed information about any finishing steps, refer to "Finishing Your Quilt" (page 31).

1. To make the backing, sew the 6" square to one end of the 6" × 40" strip to make a strip that's 6" × 45½". Sew the strip to the long side of the 40" × 45½" rectangle to make a backing that measures 45½" square.

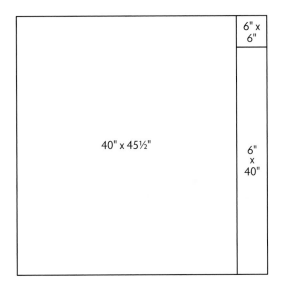

Make a 45½" square backing.

2. Layer the quilt top, batting, and backing; baste the layers together.

3. Quilt. The sample shown is machine quilted using cream thread around each star shape and in an allover grid pattern in the background. Red thread is used to stitch straight lines from point to point through each Star.

4. Make, sign, and date a label and attach it to the back of your quilt.

5. Join the 2¼"-wide fabric C strips end to end to make one long strip. Bind the quilt edges by hand or machine using the pieced strip.

Dot
Cut 13 from fabric C.

Pattern does not include seam allowances.

Churn Dash Table Topper

------- ✂ -------

FINISHED QUILT SIZE: 34½" × 34½"
FINISHED BLOCK SIZE: 12" × 12"

For this table topper, we'll set the blocks with sashing. You'll master the technique of watching for the triangle points as you sew so you don't stitch over them when joining the blocks and sashing.

Materials

Yardage is based on 42"-wide fabric.

½ yard of white solid (fabric A) for block backgrounds

⅜ yard of green print (fabric B) for Churn Dashes

½ yard of gray print (fabric C) for sashing and binding

⅝ yard of yellow floral (fabric D) for cornerstone and border

1⅛ yards of backing fabric

39" × 39" piece of batting

Cutting

From the white solid (fabric A), cut:

1 strip, 5" × 42"; crosscut into 8 squares, 5" × 5"

2 strips, 4½" × 42"; crosscut into:
- 16 rectangles, 2½" × 4½"
- 4 squares, 4½" × 4½"

From the green print (fabric B), cut:

1 strip, 5" × 42"; crosscut into 8 squares, 5" × 5"

1 strip, 4½" × 42"; crosscut into 16 rectangles, 2½" × 4½"

From the gray print (fabric C), cut:

2 strips, 2½" × 42"; crosscut into 4 strips, 2½" × 12½"

4 strips, 2¼" × 42"

From the yellow floral (fabric D), cut:

2 strips, 4½" × 26½"

2 strips, 4½" × 34½"

1 square, 2½" × 2½"

Making the Blocks

Use a ¼" seam allowance throughout. After sewing each seam, press the seam allowances in the directions indicated by the arrows. For detailed instructions and photos, refer to "Block 6: Churn Dash" (page 50).

1. Join 2½" × 4½" rectangles of fabric A and fabric B along one long edge to make a rail unit. The unit should measure 4½" square, including seam allowance. Make 16 units.

Make 16 units,
4½" x 4½".

2. Draw a diagonal line from corner to corner on the wrong side of each 5" fabric A square. Place each marked square on a 5" fabric B square, right sides together and edges aligned. Stitch ¼" from each side of the drawn line. Cut the squares apart on the marked line to make two half-square-triangle units. Press and trim the units to measure 4½" square. Make a total of 16 units.

Make 16 units,
4½" x 4½".

3. Lay out four half-square-triangle units, four rail units, and one fabric A 4½" square in three rows, rotating the units as shown.

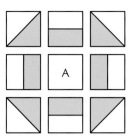

4. Sew the pieces together into rows. Join the rows to complete a Churn Dash block. The block should measure 12½" square, including seam allowances. Make a total of four blocks.

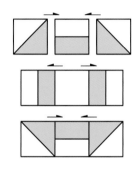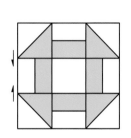

Make 4 blocks,
12½" x 12½".

Assembling the Table Topper

1. Join two blocks and one 2½" × 12½" fabric C strip as shown to make a block row. The row should measure 12½" × 26½", including seam allowances. Make two rows.

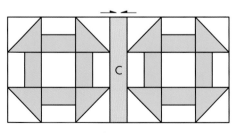

Make 2 rows,
12½" x 26½".

2. Join two 2½" × 12½" fabric C strips and the fabric D square as shown to make a sashing row. The row should measure 2½" × 26½", including seam allowances.

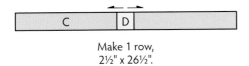

Make 1 row,
2½" x 26½".

3. Join the block rows and sashing row as shown in the table-topper assembly diagram below to complete the table-topper center, which should measure 26½" square, including seam allowances.

4. Sew 4½" × 26½" fabric D strips to opposite sides of the table topper. Sew 4½" × 34½" fabric D strips to the top and bottom of the table topper to complete the border. The table topper should measure 34½" square, including seam allowances.

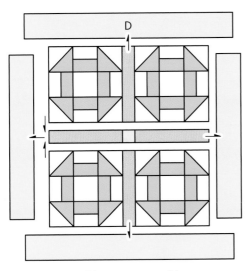

Table-topper assembly

Finishing the Table Topper

For more detailed information about any finishing steps, refer to "Finishing Your Quilt" (page 31).

1. **Cut the backing fabric** to make a backing approximately 4" longer and wider than the table topper.

2. **Layer the table topper,** batting, and backing; baste the layers together.

3. **Quilt.** The sample shown is machine quilted using gray thread in an allover pattern of wavy lines from top to bottom.

4. **Make, sign, and date a label** and attach it to the back of your table topper.

5. **Join the fabric C 2¼"-wide strips** end to end to make one long strip. Bind the quilt edges by hand or machine using the pieced strip.

Sawtooth Star Table Topper

------- ✂ ------

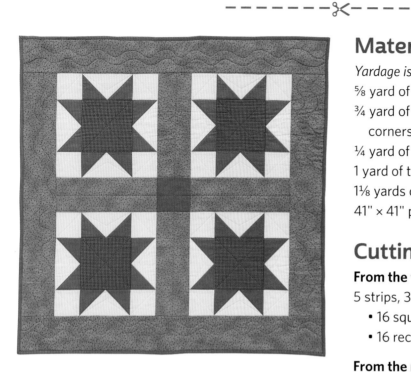

FINISHED QUILT SIZE: 36½" × 36½"
FINISHED BLOCK SIZE: 12" × 12"

While making this table topper, you'll master making star-point units. A simple yet lively table topper, this pattern looks great in any fabric. Make one for each season to keep your table stylish all year long.

Materials

Yardage is based on 42"-wide fabric.
⅝ yard of white solid (fabric A) for blocks
¾ yard of red solid (fabric B) for blocks, sashing cornerstone, and binding
¼ yard of brown check (fabric C) for blocks
1 yard of tan print (fabric D) for sashing and border
1⅛ yards of fabric for backing
41" × 41" piece of batting

Cutting

From the white solid (fabric A), cut:
5 strips, 3½" × 42"; crosscut into:
- 16 squares, 3½" × 3½"
- 16 rectangles, 3½" × 6½"

From the red solid (fabric B), cut:
3 strips, 3½" × 42"; crosscut into 32 squares, 3½" × 3½"
4 strips, 2¼" × 42"
1 square, 4½" × 4½"

From the brown check (fabric C), cut:
1 strip, 6½" × 42"; crosscut into 4 squares, 6½" × 6½"

From the tan print (fabric D), cut:
2 strips, 4½" × 42"; crosscut into 4 strips, 4½" × 12½"
2 strips, 4½" × 28½"
2 strips, 4½" × 36½"

Making the Blocks

Use a ¼" seam allowance throughout. After sewing each seam, press the seam allowances in the directions indicated by the arrows. For detailed instructions and photos, refer to "Block 7: Sawtooth Star" (page 53).

1. **Draw a diagonal line** from corner to corner on the wrong side of each 3½" fabric B square. Pin a marked square on one end of a 3½" × 6½" fabric A rectangle, right sides together and raw edges aligned. Sew along the line, one thin thread's width from the line, on what will be the seam allowance side of the line. Trim away the excess corner fabric, leaving a ¼" seam allowance.

2. **Place a second marked square** on the other end of the rectangle, right sides together and raw edges aligned. Sew, press, and trim as before. Make a total of 16 star-point units. Each unit should measure 3½" × 6½", including seam allowances.

Make 16 units,
3½" x 6½".

3. **Lay out four star-point units,** four 3½" fabric A squares, and one 6½" fabric C square in three rows, making sure to rotate the star-point units as shown.

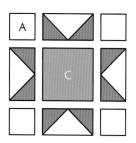

4. **Sew the pieces together** into rows. Press. Join the rows to complete a Sawtooth Star block and press. The block should measure 12½" square, including seam allowances. Make four blocks.

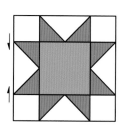
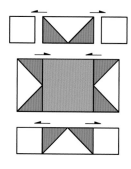

Make 4 blocks,
12½" x 12½".

See the Points

Whenever possible, sew with the star-point unit on top of the square. That way you'll be able to see the X intersection on the flying-geese unit and you'll know where to sew so you don't cut off the point.

Assembling the Table Topper

1. **Join two blocks** and one 4½" × 12½" fabric D strip as shown to make a block row. Press. The row should measure 12½" × 28½", including seam allowances. Make two rows.

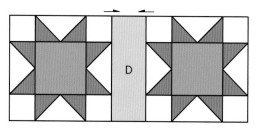

Make 2 rows,
12½" x 28½".

2. Join two 4½" × 12½" fabric D strips and the 4½" fabric B square as shown to make a sashing row. The row should measure 4½" × 28½", including seam allowances.

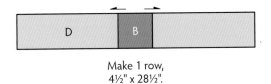

Make 1 row,
4½" x 28½".

3. Join the block rows and sashing row as shown in the table-topper assembly diagram below to complete the table-topper center, which should measure 28½" square, including seam allowances. Press.

4. Sew the 4½" × 28½" fabric D strips to opposite sides of the table topper. Press. Sew the 4½" × 36½" fabric D strips to the top and bottom of the table topper to complete the border; press. The table topper should measure 36½" square, including seam allowances.

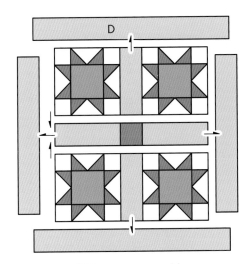

Table-topper assembly

Finishing the Table Topper

For more detailed information about any finishing steps, refer to "Finishing Your Quilt" (page 31).

1. Trim the selvages from the backing fabric and press. There's no need to piece the backing.

2. Layer the table topper, batting, and backing; baste the layers together.

3. Quilt. In the sample shown, the block background is machine quilted using white thread and straight lines. Red thread is used to stitch in the ditch around the star points. Straight lines are quilted in the center square to form an X using tan thread. Straight lines are quilted through the sashing and two evenly spaced wavy lines are quilted in the border.

4. Make, sign, and date a label and attach it to the back of your table topper.

5. Join the 2¼"-wide fabric B strips end to end to make one long strip. Bind the quilt edges by hand or machine using the pieced strip.

Hip to Be Square Table Runner

✂

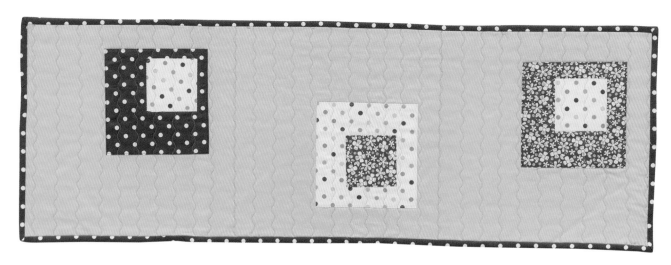

FINISHED QUILT SIZE: 12½" × 36½"
FINISHED BLOCK SIZE: 12" × 12"

For this table runner, you'll set the blocks side by side, rotating them to create a fun layout. I didn't include a border, which makes the table runner a quick and easy project.

Materials

Yardage is based on 42"-wide fabric. Fat eighths measure 9" × 21".

½ yard of peach solid (fabric A) for block backgrounds

1 fat eighth of white dot (fabric B) for appliquéd squares

1 fat eighth of gray floral (fabric C) for appliquéd squares

½ yard of brown dot (fabric D) for appliquéd square and binding

⅝ yard of fabric for backing

17" × 41" piece of batting

¾ yard of paper-backed fusible web

Cutting

From the peach solid (fabric A), cut:
3 squares, 13" × 13"

From the brown dot (fabric D), cut:
3 strips, 2¼" × 42"

Making the Blocks

For detailed instructions and photos, refer to "Block 8: Hip to Be Square" (page 57).

1. Referring to "Easy Fusible Appliqué" (page 25) and using the patterns (page 60), trace each square three times onto the fusible web. Roughly cut out the squares, leaving ½" beyond the drawn line. Cut through the excess web around each

square, through the marked line, and into the interior of the square. Then cut away the excess fusible web on the *inside* of each square, leaving less than ¼" inside the drawn line.

2. Position one large and two small fusible-web squares on the wrong side of the fabric B. Place one large and one small fusible-web square on the wrong side of the fabric C. Place one large fusible-web square on the wrong side of the fabric D. Fuse the squares as instructed by the manufacturer. Using a ruler and rotary cutter, cut out each square on the marked lines. Remove the paper backing from each square.

3. Place a 13" fabric A background square on your ironing board, right side up. Position a prepared large square in the upper-right section of the background square, making sure to place the square at least ¾" from the outer edges of the fabric A square. Place a prepared small square on top of the large square. Fuse the squares in place. Straight stitch around the outer edges of each square using a matching or contrasting thread. Referring to "Squaring Up Blocks" (page 23), trim the block to measure 12½" square, including the seam allowances. Make a total of three appliquéd blocks.

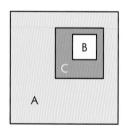

Make 2 blocks,
12½" x 12½".

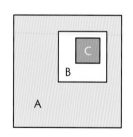

Make 1 block,
12½" x 12½".

Assembling the Table Runner

Using a ¼" seam allowance and rotating the blocks as desired, sew the blocks together side by side to make a table runner that measures 12½" × 36½", including seam allowances. Press the seam allowances in one direction.

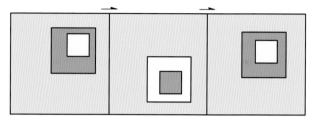

Table-runner assembly

Finishing the Table Runner

For more detailed information about any finishing steps, refer to "Finishing Your Quilt" (page 31).

1. Cut the backing fabric so it's approximately 4" longer and wider than the table runner.

2. Layer the table runner, batting, and backing; baste the layers together.

3. Quilt. The sample shown is machine quilted using peach thread in an allover pattern of wavy lines from side to side.

4. Make, sign, and date a label and attach it to the back of your table runner.

5. Join the 2¼"-wide fabric D strips end to end to make one long strip. Bind the quilt edges by hand or machine using the pieced strip.

Beautiful Bloom Table Runner

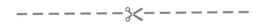

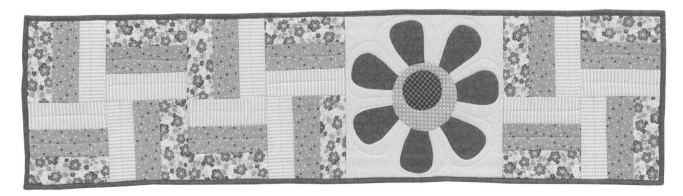

FINISHED QUILT SIZE: 12½" × 48½"
FINISHED BLOCK SIZE: 12" × 12"

I combined three Rail Fence blocks and a Beautiful Bloom block to make this sweet table runner.

Materials

Yardage is based on 42"-wide fabric.

¼ yard of tan stripe (fabric A) for Rail Fence blocks
¼ yard of tan dot (fabric B) for Rail Fence blocks
¼ yard of red floral (fabric C) for Rail Fence blocks
½ yard of red print (fabric D) for petals and binding
6" × 6" square of tan print (fabric E) for large circle
4" × 4" square of red check (fabric F) for small circle
13" × 13" square of cream solid (fabric G) for
    Beautiful Bloom block
1⅛ yards of fabric for backing
17" × 53" piece of batting

Cutting

From the tan stripe (fabric A), cut:
2 strips, 2½" × 42"; crosscut into 12 rectangles,
    2½" × 6½"

From the tan dot (fabric B), cut:
2 strips, 2½" × 42"; crosscut into 12 rectangles,
    2½" × 6½"

From the red floral (fabric C), cut:
2 strips, 2½" × 42"; crosscut into 12 rectangles,
    2½" × 6½"

From the red print (fabric D), cut:
4 strips, 2¼" × 42"

Making the Rail Fence Blocks

Use a ¼" seam allowance throughout. After sewing each seam, press the seam allowances in the directions indicated by the arrows. For detailed instructions and photos, refer to "Block 2: Rail Fence" (page 39).

1. Join a fabric A, a fabric B, and a fabric C rectangle along their long edges to make a 6½" square unit, including seam allowances. Make 12 units.

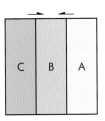

Make 12 units,
6½" x 6½".

2. Lay out the units from step 1 as shown. Sew the units together into rows. Join the rows to complete a Rail Fence block. The block should measure 12½" square, including seam allowances. Make a total of three blocks.

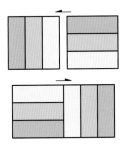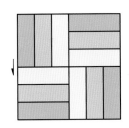

Make 3 blocks,
12½" x 12½".

Making the Beautiful Bloom Block

For detailed instructions and photos, refer to "Block 9: Beautiful Bloom" (page 61) and "Easy Fusible Appliqué" (page 25) as needed throughout.

1. **Using the patterns (page 64)**, trace the number of shapes indicated on the patterns onto the fusible web. Roughly cut out each shape, leaving ½" beyond the drawn line. Cut through the excess web around each shape, through the marked line, and into the interior of the shape. Then cut away the excess fusible web on the *inside* of each shape, leaving less than ¼" inside the drawn line.

2. **Position the fusible-web shapes** on the wrong side of the fabrics as follows: petals on fabric D, large circle on fabric E, and small circle on fabric F. Fuse as instructed by the manufacturer. Cut out each prepared appliqué shape on the marked lines. Remove the paper backing from each shape.

3. **Place the 13" fabric G background square** on your ironing board, right side up. Position the prepared shapes on the background square as described on page 62. Fuse the shapes in place. Straight stitch around the outer edges of each shape using a matching or contrasting thread. Referring to "Squaring Up Blocks" (page 23),

trim the block to measure 12½" square, including seam allowances.

Make 1 block,
12½" x 12½".

Assembling the Table Runner

Using a ¼" seam allowance, sew the Rail Fence and Beautiful Bloom blocks together side by side to make a table runner that measures 12½" × 48½", including seam allowance. Press.

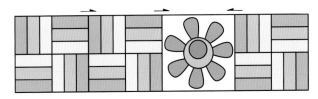

Table-runner assembly

Finishing the Table Runner

For more detailed information about any finishing steps, refer to "Finishing Your Quilt" (page 31).

1. **Cut the backing fabric** into two 17" × 40" rectangles and sew them together end to end to make a backing approximately 4" longer and wider than the table runner.

2. **Layer the table runner**, batting, and backing; baste the layers together.

3. **Quilt.** The sample shown is machine quilted using cream thread and straight lines in the Rail Fence blocks. Stitch in the ditch around the appliqué shapes in the Beautiful Bloom block and then echo quilt the petals.

4. **Make, sign, and date a label** and attach it to the back of your table runner.

5. **Join the 2¼"-wide fabric D strips** end to end to make one long strip. Bind the quilt edges by hand or machine using the pieced strip.

I'm a quilt designer, author, teacher, radio/ podcast show producer and host, and fabric designer. My passion for making quilts, sharing quilts, and talking with quilters about quilts is limitless. I travel across the world teaching and host several Internet groups of quilters where we share what we make on a daily basis. I also write about quilting on my blog. To find me, go to www.PatSloan.com, sign up for my newsletter, and let's chat soon!

Acknowledgments

Many thanks to:

Melaine Barrett, Roberta Miglin, Lina LaMora, Cindy Dickinson, and Dennis Dickinson, who helped me meet stitching deadlines.

I also work with amazing partners in the industry:

♦ Moda Fabrics not only prints my fabric line, but their fabrics are the ones I tend to hoard the most. Plus, they shared wonderful props to make the photos in this book delightful.

♦ Aurifil creates beautiful-quality thread in a delicious array of colors that I love.

♦ Thanks to the Tacony Corporation for the Baby Lock sewing machine I use at home and in the photos in this book.

♦ Therm O Web makes the most consistent and dependable fusible web, HeatnBond Lite.

♦ Mountain Mist battings add the best middle layer to my quilts.

♦ Reliable manufactures irons that live up to their name.

♦ Olfa makes the best rotary cutter ever.